Up 'n' Under I

A play

John Godber

Samuel French — London
New York - Toronto - Hollywood

UP 'N' UNDER II

First performed at the Hull Truck Theatre, Hull, in
November 1993, with the following cast:

Arthur	Nigel Betts
Frank	David Telfo
Steve	Nick Lane
Phil	Dan O'Brian
Spud	Adrian Hood
Hazel	Susan Cookson
Doreen	Susan Cookson
Ray Mason	David Telfo
Reg Welsh	Dan O'Brian

Directed by John Godber
Designed by Liam Doona
Music by Chris Madin

CHARACTERS

Steve
Phil
Frank
Arthur
Hazel
Ray Mason
Reg Welsh
Spud
Doreen

SYNOPSIS OF SCENES

Time — the present

Other plays by John Godber
published by Samuel French Ltd:

April in Paris
Happy Families
Salt of the Earth
Teechers
Up 'n' Under

ACT I

SCENE 1

Musical overture

A playing field in front of a notional "clubhouse"

The Lights come up. It is night and perishingly cold. The cold wind howls. Several rugby balls lie on the ground, along with Arthur's sports bag

Steve, Phil, Frank, Arthur and Hazel are training, throwing a rugby ball about listlessly. They are completely frozen and caked with mud; they cut a very sorry picture. They look as if they almost don't believe they are actually training in weather like this. Arthur is attempting to get them to train harder

Arthur Come on, come on ... move it. Come on Phil, Frank ... Come on lads, come on, keep moving, move that ball about, don't let the cold get to you.
Steve It's got to me.
Arthur Twenty press-ups, Steve. Come on, come on, keep working.
Steve Twenty press-ups?
Arthur Give me twenty, Stevie.
Steve I'll give you five. (*He does five press-ups*)
Arthur Come on, lads, it's not cold.
Phil Isn't it?
Arthur Well done Hazel, swing that ball about. Keep them hands warm.
Steve Are we calling that it, then, or what?
Phil Let's call that it, Arthur.
Arthur Another four times round the field, eh?
Phil We can't pick our legs up.
Arthur Twice around the field, eh lads? Then we'll call that it.
Phil We're ossifying here ...
Frank We're frozen to the marrow, Arthur.
Arthur Hazel, what about you, another game of touch and pass?
Hazel I think we've done enough for one night.

There is a pause

Steve So is that it, then, or what?
Arthur You don't want to pack in, do you, Steve?

Frank He never wanted to come out.

Steve I can't feel owt, me, I could be dead from the waist down.

Hazel Yeah, that's what I've heard.

Phil My teeth are chattering.

Hazel I thought I could hear something ...

Phil How long have we been out here?

Steve Six hours.

Phil You're joking.

Steve It could be longer; my watch has frozen up.

Arthur All right then, lads. Nice one; we'll call that it for tonight.

Frank It's about time.

Steve Alleluia.

Hazel Everybody get a good bath, a good soak.

Steve Is that an offer?

Arthur Well done everybody, nice one lads, well done. We're looking good.

Phil We're actually dying of frost-bite. You know that the showers don't work, Arthur, don't you? I wouldn't send kids home like this. It's a disgrace.

Steve I'm not showering in this.

Frank Put a sock in it, Phil, will you?

Phil These were all clean on tonight.

Arthur And be careful with your valuables. I don't think things are safe in there.

Frank Nothing's safe around here, Arthur.

Phil We lose a ball every game.

Frank We had the telly nicked once.

Phil And we were watching it at the time.

Steve Whose bloody daft idea was it to play 'em again anyway?

Hazel Guess.

Arthur Double or quits; we all agreed on that.

Steve That was nearly nine months ago in the heat of the battle. Emotions were running high ... I mean, I can't remember anything about it.

Arthur Well, I can. You said you were in for it. We all did.

Frank Come on, it'll be a laugh.

Steve It wasn't much of a laugh last time, was it?

Arthur Come on, Steve, up and at 'em.

Hazel You played well last time, didn't you?

Frank He even scored. That's your first try in thirty games.

Hazel Come on, Steve, where are your guts?

Phil Don't ask.

Steve I know, but at Christmas? I've got all my Christmas shopping to do yet. I haven't bought a bloody thing.

Arthur I wouldn't worry, Steve, it's late opening this week.

Steve Arthur, you are clinically insane.

Hazel It's a laugh though, Steve.

Steve What is?

Hazel That noise you make at the back of your throat, that's a laugh.

Phil She's catching on.

Steve We're all dying of pneumonia and Hazel's telling jokes. I rest my case, your worship. Totally loony, the load of 'em.

Frank Eye of the tiger, eh, Hazel?

Hazel That's right.

Steve Eye of the tiger? I've got the eye of a worm.

Phil And you've got the face of a pig, so that should be interesting.

Arthur See you all Wednesday, then.

Steve I'll tell you sommat: if it's like this I'm not coming, so sit on that.

Arthur I'll phone up the weather centre, Steve, and get a forecast for you.

Steve If it's like this, count me out.

Arthur He'll be here.

Steve I can think of a million more interesting things to do than run about in this lot. Now some of you might not be able to, and for you this might be the most exciting thing in your sorry lives. And I'm happy for you. But not for me.

Phil Oooh, he's touchy tonight.

Frank Must be on a promise.

Hazel Who is she, Steve?

Steve Sorry Hazel, you wouldn't know her.

Phil And you do?

Steve Let's just say I'm going to.

Frank Not funny but fast.

Arthur And not all that fast from what I've seen.

Steve I'm faster than you.

Arthur You what? I'll have you now, twice round the field.

Steve Oh that old joke, and I nearly believed you. I was nearly off like a wet whippet. Arthur, I'd beat you with one leg.

Hazel Could get arrested for that, beating somebody with one leg.

Steve You're funny, Hazel, you know that. For a woman.

Frank Hey, no need to be nasty.

Arthur Sounds like one of Phil's jokes.

Phil One of Frank's, more like.

Frank Right then Steve, I'll drop you at the *Wheatsheaf*.

Steve Superb.

Hazel You're not meeting her there, are you?

Steve Yeah, and we're going out to a fancy dress like this. I'm gonna get a bath. If he lets me.

Arthur He's in with the landlord.

Frank I've got to nip the kids' Christmas presents down first.
Steve They still believe in Father Christmas, Frank?
Frank Why, don't you?
Steve Course I do. I've sent a hundred notes up our chimney this year already.
Frank I can't do that any more.
Steve Why, have you got central heating?
Frank No, they're at their mother's now. First Christmas on my own ...
    Anyway, I'll see you later.
Steve Come on, Frank. Hey, Hazel, give him a kiss, cheer him up a bit.
Hazel He's all right, aren't you, Frank?
Frank Ar.

*Frank and Steve exit into the clubhouse. Hazel collects the balls to take
them into the clubhouse*

Arthur (*calling after Frank and Steve*) Wednesday.
Steve (*off*) I'm not coming.

Pause

Arthur You're all right for Wednesday, aren't you, Phil?
Phil I think Steve may have a point.
Arthur I'm not talking about training. I thought we might have a bit of a
    social night.
Hazel Another?

Hazel exits to the clubhouse

Arthur Just a few drinks and few videos.
Phil Sorry to disappoint, Arth, but I've gone teetotal.
Arthur Thought it might be good to boost morale.
Phil Get legless, you mean?
Arthur Well, it's the season, isn't it? You know, have a bit of a do.
Phil Listen, Arthur, I enjoy playing, and I don't mind training, no matter what
    the weather. But I think I could live without seeing another *Rocky* video.
Arthur Who mentioned *Rocky*?
Phil You don't have to.
Arthur I never mentioned *Rocky*.
Phil Every time we have a social do we all end up watching *Rocky*. You're
    Rocky mad.
Arthur You don't watch 'em, you go home. Come on, Phil. It's harmless
    stuff.
Phil Is it?

Arthur It'll boost morale, pick us up a bit.
Phil So you think we need it, then?
Arthur I think we need to be a team, Phil.
Phil I think a team needs more players.
Arthur We'll get 'em. Aren't there any big lads at school?
Phil It's a Rugby Union school.
Arthur A couple of sixth formers could be handy.
Phil We need a game plan.
Arthur We did all right last time.
Phil It was a bloody fluke.
Arthur Get away, we played out of our skins.
Phil And there's nothing left.
Arthur We did.
Phil I know.
Arthur So we'll do it again.
Phil These lads'll never do that again, Arth. It's a once in a lifetime performance.
Arthur They will — we all will.
Phil You reckon?
Arthur You trust me.
Phil Trust you? You mean like last time? We only found out about the bloody bet by accident. Trust you?
Arthur We'll do it.
Phil I don't know why, but I don't believe you.
Arthur You've got to believe me. And if you don't, don't tell me that you don't believe me. Lie to me, Phil. I can take lying to.
Phil Arthur, you're a bloody education.
Arthur Speaking of which, if you've never seen *Rocky* it'll be an education for you.
Phil This team are great on jokes and poor on ball play.
Arthur Have a good night. I might catch you later. Have a word with Steve; will you get him to bring his video? He'll love it when he hears we're not training.

Phil exits

Arthur has a moment on his own. He hugs himself against the cold, and goes through a few kicking motions

Hazel returns from the clubhouse, now wearing a winter anorak. She looks at Arthur; she senses a change in his mood

Hazel What's up?

Arthur Oh. Nothing.

Hazel Oh, I see.

Arthur Phil.

Hazel What about him?

Arthur I've got a feeling he's going to do a Tony on me.

Hazel Tony left because he lost his job, it had nothing to do with you. They said they were closing the pit and they closed it and that was it. He did what was best for him, took his redundancy money and went to seek his fortune. I think he's in Canada or somewhere. Lucky sod.

Arthur Cold, though.

Hazel Phil's all right.

Arthur You like him, don't you?

Hazel He's a good bloke.

Arthur But he's such a snob.

Hazel He's a decent player.

Arthur I know that. He's not one of us, not one of the lads.

Hazel And I am?

Arthur Your heart's in it.

Hazel We need him.

Arthur Ar. I know. He's losing it though. If they all start thinking like Phil, I'm snookered.

Hazel You know his wife's expecting?

Arthur No, I didn't.

Hazel Any day now.

Arthur Yeah, well ... It looks like he's having it for her.

Hazel He's a sensitive bloke, is Phil.

Arthur Bloody hell, Hazel, I wish I'd never agreed to do this.

Hazel It'll be all right.

Arthur Will it?

Hazel What have we got to lose?

Arthur Well, in case you've forgotten, I've got my life savings.

Hazel Yeah, well, fair point.

Arthur I'm frozen.

Hazel I'd better get off. I've got to lock the gym up.

Arthur Too much gym work makes 'em soft, you know.

Hazel I know that. If Steve stays in the gym he gets ball shy.

Arthur Oh. Is that what it is?

There is a pause

Hazel Well, another Christmas on my lonesome!

Arthur Ar well.

Hazel I hate it.

Arthur And me. Everybody is supposed to have a great time and if you don't there's something wrong with you. I have a great time three hundred and sixty days a year. I like to have Christmas off.

Hazel How's Doreen taken all this?

Arthur Ah, you don't want to know about me and my domestic life.

Hazel At least you've got somebody.

Arthur Yeah, that's right, bless her. She knows I go off the deep end. She's known me for long enough. You know, secretly I think she was pleased when we came so close. She's a diamond, is Doreen. If there is any one woman in the world who understands me, Hazel, it's her. I've done some daft things, and this takes the biscuit, but she'll always stand by me, and I'm lucky, I suppose.

Hazel Certainly are.

Arthur Her dad ran a pub team in Normanton. Their Pete had trials for Leeds. It's part of her life.

Hazel It's in the blood then, is it?

Arthur Oh ay. In fact both families have been involved with Rugby League. My grandad, you know, was at the *George Hotel* in Huddersfield in eighteen-ninety-five, when they first formed the game. Tommy Hoyle was there. I was so proud of that. My grandad being one of the founders of Rugby League. Then I found out that he wasn't actually in the meeting room; he was downstairs in the smoke room propping the bar up. Ar ... the stuff of life, Hazel. Another "if only".

There is a pause

Hazel I'll have to get off, Arthur.

Arthur You be OK going home alone?

Hazel Yeah.

Arthur Must get lonely, nights like this?

Hazel Well, I'm hardly ever there, am I? I'm training.

Arthur Sorry to get you involved in all this, Hazel.

Hazel I love it. What else would I be doing? Timing some overweight business man on an exercise bike? Been there, done that.

Arthur There aren't any other women down at the gym who'd fancy a game, are there?

Hazel Don't think so. I could ask. Hey, what about Doreen, couldn't you get her to turn out for us? If it's in the family she might be just what we're looking for?

Arthur No, I just can't see that somehow.

Hazel I'd like to meet her.

Arthur (*sarcastically*) Yeah, that'd be nice.

Hazel Anyway ...

Arthur You'd better get off.
Hazel I'll race you to the cars.
Arthur I think my legs have seized up.
Hazel Come on, Arthur ... you're acting like an old man.

She jogs off easily

Arthur (*picking up his bag*) That's right Hazel, it's all an act. I'm as fit as a butcher's dog, really.

Arthur pulls on his hat and awkwardly jogs off

Music plays

The Lights fade to Black-out

SCENE 2

The same. Some days later

The Lights come up. It is a crisp winter morning with frost in the air and on the ground

Ray Mason, a local radio sports reporter, enters from the clubhouse carrying a tape recorder. Reg Welsh is with him

Ray Won't keep you a moment, Reg.
Reg Good.
Ray (*into the tape recorder*) This is Ray Mason. This is "Sports Scene". This is Ray Mason, this is "Sports Scene". Hallo, hallo.
Reg Hallo.
Ray (*to Reg*) No, I was just saying hallo to this. (*Into the tape recorder*) Testing testing, one two, one two. Is it working, this? Hallo. Yeah ... Yeah ... Well, it's working, anyway.
Reg Lovely.
Ray (*into the tape recorder*) This is Ray Mason, this is "Sports Scene", and this is a "Sports Scene Special". There's always been rivalry between the great teams of the North. Hull versus Cas, Wigan versus Leeds; great teams, great fixtures. Of course any talk about Rugby League will bring out loyalties and prejudice. But never has the rivalry been so fierce as here on Walton fields in Humberside. Almost nine months ago now the plucky amateurs from the *Wheatsheaf Arms* took on and narrowly lost to the *Cobblers* from Castleford. The *Cobblers* of course are the unbeaten sevens

champions, veritable giants in the amateur arena. I've got Reg Welsh with me, their manager and no stranger to the "Sports Scene" programme. Bit of a shock, Reg?

Ray interviews Reg with the tape recorder

During the interview, Arthur enters rather sheepishly

Reg They played well, Ray. I can't take that away from 'em. But we made some silly mistakes.

Ray Why a re-match?

Reg They wanted one, Ray. I think the crowd wanted one. And I wanted to put the record straight and beat 'em good and proper this time.

Ray There's a lot of passion in the amateur game, Reg?

Reg Of course there is, it's the breeding ground for talented youngsters, and it's a place where the older player can sort of live out his retirement, if you like.

Ray Reg, you've played professionally: what does it mean to these lads to turn out after a day's work and play Rugby League?

Reg Well they're good as gold, some of these lads, Ray. They look forward to the simple things in life. A pint, a game, a clash of heads, a bloody nose.

Ray It's going to be a great day for Rugby League.

Reg It'll be a party, Ray, I can assure you of that.

Ray Pride and a trophy to play for, honour, love of the game and not a little cash at stake. Reg, any plans if you win?

Reg No "if" about it, Ray. The *Cobblers* are a dead cert.

Ray You're that certain?

Reg I'm that certain Ray, we've already pledged that money to the Children in Need Appeal.

Ray That's lovely.

Reg In fact, Ray, I've given the *Cobblers* a few days' rest from training. I'm letting my lads enjoy the build-up.

Ray waves Arthur over

Ray You sound very confident.

Reg Lambs to the slaughter, Ray.

Ray Well, we've just been joined by Arthur Hoyle, ex-Wakefield Trinity, and now trainer of the *Wheatsheaf Arms*. What do you make of that, Arthur?

Arthur Well, that's what they said last time.

Ray Are you lambs to the slaughter?

Arthur They'll not beat us, I'll tell you that much.

Ray Very unlucky last time, Arthur: a last-minute penalty and you hit the crossbar.

Arthur All that's behind us now, we're just looking forward to the game.

Ray Training going well?

Arthur Couldn't be better.

Ray Weather no problem? Bitterly cold at the moment.

Arthur The lads love it. They can't wait to train.

Ray Reg is very confident, Arthur. How do you respond to that?

Arthur Well, he'll probably bring some ringers in, that's what they did last time.

Reg Steady on.

Arthur If the *Cobblers* fielded seven amateurs it'd be a miracle. They've not done it yet and I've been watching 'em for five years.

Reg They were all amateurs.

Arthur Half the *Cobblers* team were in the Castleford Reserves the week before and he knows it's true.

Reg Go steady, you.

Arthur They even brought in somebody from Warrington.

Reg He'd had trials for Workington. Get your facts right. He played with us as a youth player.

Arthur I wouldn't be surprised if half the Great Britain squad turned out for 'em on Boxing Day.

Ray Reg, anything to add to that ?

Reg It's blokes like this that give Rugby League a bad name. He's trying to keep the game back in the seventies. Things have changed, the game's changed.

Arthur Ask him how much he's getting for commentating on Sky TV, ask him that. That's what's changed.

Reg What's that got to do with this? Listen, you were lucky we didn't wipe the floor with you last time. You'll not be so lucky this time. You'd better get your cheque book out.

Arthur He's only interested in the money.

Reg Get your cheque book out, Arthur.

Arthur We'll beat you.

Reg You couldn't beat an egg.

Arthur We'll see.

Reg We will.

Arthur I'll have you now.

Reg What, are you bloody crackers?

Ray Wow, steady hang on ... Now wait on.

Arthur Why don't you put some money back into the game, Reg, instead of pocketing it all?

Reg He shares a brain this bloke ——

Ray Can we just hang on?

Reg — and it's not his turn to have it this week.

Arthur Go on, man, you're not worth talking to.

Reg You're bloody barmy, man.

Arthur Put your money into the game, Reg, not your bank account.

Reg You're a disgrace to the game, Arthur.

Reg exits

Arthur looks flustered

Ray (*desperate to save the tape*) Well, remarkable scenes. Temperatures certainly running high. I said, passions were aroused. Obviously a hint of healthy rivalry between the two managers. Is that right, Arthur?

Arthur Well, it's just hot air really, Ray. It'll all be decided on the day.

Ray But Arthur, aren't you really trying to make a silk purse from a pig's ear?

Arthur I am trying to train a team of decent lads, and give them some pride in the area.

Ray And aren't you promoting the cloth cap image of the game?

Arthur I'm not bothered about the image. I just want to see good Rugby League played like it should be played. I want to show that these so-called "super sides" like the *Cobblers* can be beaten, and to give heart to any teams who have lost their drive.

Ray And will you be fielding a full squad for the game?

Arthur All being well.

Ray How many players do you have at the moment?

Arthur Five.

Ray Just five.

Arthur Just five Ray, yes, but all extremely talented players.

Ray Including a woman?

Arthur Yes.

Ray Will you be bringing in any more women?

Arthur Who knows the secret of the Black Magic box, Ray? We did hold a very successful pie and pea supper in order to boost our squad, but as yet we haven't reaped the dividends.

Ray So you're still looking for players?

Arthur Yes, always on the look-out for new talent, so if there are any brave hearts out there who fancy a game against the *Cobblers Arms* we'll be holding a special training session outside the clubhouse on Friday.

Ray Arthur, I'm sure somebody out there fancies a game. Whatever happens, it's going to be a great day for Rugby League. It's been a pleasure speaking with you, and may the best team win.

Music

The Lights fade to Black-out

SCENE 3

The interior of the clubhouse. The following Wednesday

The Lights come up, bringing a much warmer feel to the stage than we have hitherto witnessed, though the room is very sparse

Phil and Steve enter. Phil is carrying a number of seats while Steve wrestles with a video player, connecting it to the TV DR. During the early dialogue Phil exits and returns with an electric fire and plugs it in

Steve Come on, Phil, get that bloody heater on. It's colder in here than it is out there.

Phil What's wrong with you? Moan, moan, moan ...

Steve Listen who's talking.

Phil Oh, give it a miss, will you?.

Steve I think I've got thin blood. I hardly eat, you know, I just drink, and I still can't put any weight on.

Phil The amount of ale you put away I'm surprised you've got any blood at all.

Steve Coldest winter on record.

Phil Says who?

Steve Says me. I'm nesh.

Phil Nesh?

Steve Cold. It's a word, Phil. You should know all about words.

Phil Nesh, I'll remember that. (*He stands in front of the fire*)

Steve (*trying to get close to the fire*) I was thinking, don't you think it would be nice to get Arthur something for Christmas?

Phil What?

Steve Like a little present or sommat?

Phil Are you serious?

Steve Yes.

Phil Oh yeah, tell you what, we could have a whip-round and buy him some new ladders for his van. That'd be nice, you can wrap 'em up. Tell you what else we could do, we could decorate the clubhouse. I'll get some kids to cut out little angels holding rugby balls. I wonder if Arthur would like that?

Steve Funny.

Phil And we can have mistletoe and all kiss each other.

Steve Oh, bah, humbug.

Phil I'm not getting him anything. In fact if we don't get any more players I'm knocking it on the head, forget it, it's off, I'm away.

Steve Where's all the goodwill?

Phil No, I'm sorry, but that's what I'm doing. Besides he hasn't got us anything, has he?

Steve What about arranging this?

Phil It's your video, my electric fire, and the beer's from Stan at the *Wheatsheaf*. It was just Arthur's idea. And we all know about Arthur's ideas.

Steve I still think he might have got us sommat.

Phil He has, a load of bloody trouble.

Steve We could get him a video.

Phil He's got every video that's ever been released.

Steve Or some aftershave?

Phil Are you going soft or something? Must be the cold, Steve, it's rotting your brain cells.

Steve No, listen, fair point, I was only thinking that it would be a nice gesture from the team. Sommat for him to remember us by.

Phil Remember us by. Why, where's he going?

Steve Well, after this match you never know.

Phil I know where I'd wish he'd go.

Silence. Both men look cold

Steve Cold?

Phil Mesh.

Steve You're hogging the bloody fire, shift out.

Phil I'm not hogging it.

Steve When's she due then?

Phil Any day. She's not happy about all this lot.

Steve You should be at home.

Phil We've got her mother staying with us at the moment; I'm better off here. Anyway I've got a mobile if anything breaks — they can call me. Early Christmas present.

Steve Gi's a go.

Phil No, it's mine.

Steve Oh, right.

Phil What happened the other night, then?

Steve A bloody nightmare.

Phil I thought you had the golden touch with women?

Steve I did have. I was supposed to be meeting her after training. Nice lass, special, you know. From the posh end of Swanland. Her old man's got a restaurant.

Phil That could be useful.

Steve Ay, that's what I thought. (*He stands with his back to the fire*)

Phil We should have gone there.

Steve I thought I'd nip down to the *Wheatsheaf*. Have a swift half, get a bath and then take her out to that new Chinese on the Beverley Road.

Phil Posh for you, isn't it?

Steve It would have been if Stan had let me get a bath. He said that I owed too much on my bar bill so he wouldn't let me use his hot water.

Phil How much do you owe?

Steve Forty quid, maybe, fifty, sommat ridiculous.

Phil Oh right, so you went home for a shower, and by the time you got back to her house she didn't want to go out with you?

Steve No. I went as I was. In all my training muck. She thought it was a joke.

Phil Did she laugh?

Steve Not a lot.

Phil So you're not seeing her again, then?

Steve It looks unlikely.

Phil Come out, let's a have a go back at that end.

They change places so that Phil is now near the heater

Steve How much ale is he bringing?

Phil Five crates.

Steve I have five crates with my soup course.

Phil Is that with or without the mud pack?

Steve Five crates, that's not enough.

Phil Well everybody's driving, aren't they? He's got five crates of that alcohol-free.

Steve You what?

Phil I've not had a drink for nine months.

Steve Why?

Phil I'm supporting Carole with the birth.

Steve What for?

Phil Give it a rest.

Steve Alcohol-free?

Phil That's right.

Steve Alcohol-free? I've brought my drinking boots an' all.

Phil Tough.

Steve Oh, I'm sorry, I'm in the wrong place. I thought this was going to be a rugby club do not a book launch at the art gallery. Is he bringing some rare cheeses and organic wine? How lovely; pass me the quiche, will you?

Phil It's low-alcohol because of Hazel.

Steve She's not coming, is she?

Phil Best behaviour, so keep your pants on.

Steve That's it, I'm off to the book launch, they might have a stripper on.

Phil She's part of the team.

Steve I know, Phil, but fair's fair. I thought we were going to have a party, let our hair down, watch a few dodgy videos and get utterly wasted.

Phil Don't be pathetic.

Steve That's what rugby clubs do, Phil. The *Cobblers'*ll be into all that. But not us, no. It turns out we're all gunna play musical chairs, have some jelly and go to bed.

Phil You can still run about naked if you want, I'm sure Hazel's seen it all before.

Steve I mean, I've cancelled another date for this. Look, Hazel's a good laugh, she fits in, but I would have thought she'd have sense enough to know where she's not welcome. I mean, it's a good job I didn't organize something a bit tasty, isn't it?

Phil Hazel's all right.

Steve I'm not saying she isn't. She's just a bit frumpy for me. I mean I like the outdoor type. But I draw a line at a woman who plays rugby.

Phil There's a woman coach at school. It's catching on all over. About time too, makes showering interesting.

Steve No, it's unnatural, that. I mean, I wouldn't kick Hazel out of bed if the chance came, but I like a woman to look like a woman.

Phil Well, that's very modern, Steve.

Steve Yeah, I know.

Phil You've no idea what women have to put up with, have you?

Steve Hey, you were the one who didn't want a female trainer.

Phil That's true, but I've changed my opinion.

Steve Look, I came here for the ale and a mess about, not a lecture about equality.

Phil Well, I could think of a million and one other things that I could be doing instead of this. I've got some A level work to look at later. They're changing the bloody syllabus again next year — Zola and Balzac. The system's a bloody mess.

Steve I know that, and I'm a victim of it.

Phil And we'll be here watching the early reels of Sylvester Stallone. I should've brought a book.

Arthur enters from the bitter cold. He is carrying a crate of beer and a plastic bag full of videos

Arthur Bloody hell. It's the coldest winter on record.

Phil So I've heard.

Arthur (*indicating his bag*) The videos.

Phil And not an Ingrid Bergman in sight.

Arthur Let's get some heat on my body. Roads are bad. Sleet and rain forecast. Too cold for snow.

Phil As opposed to being too hot for snow?

Arthur Oh ar, funny. Bloody frozen.

Steve Hazel's coming, you know?

Arthur So what?

Steve Nothing, just saying.

Arthur She's on the team, isn't she?

Steve I know, but I nearly booked a snake dancer. I've got a mate who deals with all that stuff.

Arthur Good job we're not training in this, eh, Steve?

Steve I wouldn't be here.

Phil He'd be having a mud bath with a bird from Swanland.

Arthur Hey, we might get snowed in and have to eat somebody.

Phil That'd be fun, wouldn't it?

Steve Don't look at me.

Arthur We can eat Frank first.

Steve Yeah, he'd last us a month.

Phil Has that radio interview been out yet?

Arthur Some time this week. Anybody want a beer?

Steve You haven't got any low-alcohol have you?

Arthur Five crates.

Steve Fantastic, we'll probably die of zinc poisoning. (*He helps himself to a beer*)

Phil So nobody'll really hear it, will they?

Arthur What?

Phil That interview — they'll all be out getting sozzled.

Arthur You never know. No luck with the lads from school.

Phil Well they are on holiday, but I managed to track down a few sixth formers from the first team. They said they'd rather die than play against the *Cobblers*.

Steve Amounts to the same thing, doesn't it?

Arthur They're only kids anyway. Long shot, but worth it I suppose — you never know.

Phil So we're going to play with just four, are we?

Arthur Plus Hazel.

Steve (*drinking his beer*) It's not bad this, it's got one of them draught flow systems.

Phil Like Arthur's head.

Frank enters. He is wrapped against the night. His anorak hides the fact that he is wearing a very smart blazer and slacks and a shirt and tie. He carries a number of bags of goodies

Steve Yo, Frankie, get the wine gums out.

Phil Here he is. The hardest man in Hull.

Frank Sorry I'm late. I've been wrapping up some Christmas presents.

Steve Don't bother wrapping mine, Frank.

Frank I didn't.
Steve Fair enough.
Frank In fact I haven't got you one.

Frank takes off his anorak and reveals his smart attire. This creates a round of cat calls and sundry responses

Arthur Centrefold stuff, eh, Frank?
Frank I like to make the effort.
Phil This is it, you know, Frank. We're not going anywhere else, we're having the party here.
Frank Careful Phil, that was nearly funny.
Steve Frank is wearing the very latest in butcher's *haute couture*. The shirt is by Mr Ordinary of Hessle, the socks are by Wear and Stink of Hull. The tie is from the Second Draw, First Marriage House in Gilberdyke, and the slacks are by Karl Sackoshit. Aftershave: *Pig's Breath* by Ralph Lauren.
Frank He's on bloody drugs, that lad.
Steve I wish I was.
Phil *Haute couture*?
Steve *Oui, oui*, duckie.
Frank Right, anybody fancy a bit of a nibble? I've got all sorts in here. Best lean ham and all. Ham sandwiches, pork scratchings. A bit of tongue. Phil, bit of tongue?
Phil Already got one, thanks.
Frank Arthur, fancy a pig's trotter?
Arthur No thanks, Frank.
Frank There's a lot to suck on.
Arthur I fancy a bit of pork pie.
Frank I've got tripe.
Steve Tripe. Hallo, hallo, Frank, please come in, anybody there, hallo? It's nineteen-ninety-three, please do you read me?
Frank Try a bit of tripe, Stevie, it'll put hairs on your chest.
Steve I don't want hairs on my chest.
Phil What chest?
Arthur What's the occasion, Frank?
Frank Eh?
Arthur All the clobber?
Frank I haven't worn this sort of stuff since Tina walked out on me ——
Steve Look out ...
Frank — but I just saw it there in the wardrobe and I felt like putting it on.
Arthur Good for you.
Frank Right, what video you got for us then, Arth?
Phil *Babette's Feast*, by the sound of it.

Arthur *Rocky V.*
Phil Oh good, my favourite.
Arthur He'll love it, when he sees it.
Frank I've seen 'em all.
Steve I have.
Arthur I've seen 'em that many times I could be in 'em.

*Hazel enters, also wrapped against the cold in a long duffel coat. She wears
steel- rimmed glasses and looks classy*

Hazel Going to freeze over, I think. The ground's like rock.
Steve (*in a Scottish accent*) We're all doomed.
Hazel Well, this looks cosy. Home from home, eh, Arthur? No room at the
inn, so we're in here.
Phil Very good.
Arthur It'll do for me.

*Hazel takes off her coat and reveals a very sexy winter outfit. She looks unlike
the Hazel we have seen before*

Hazel Don't hog the fire, Phil, I'm frozen. (*She moves to the fire*)
Phil Mesh.
Hazel Not much. Right, that's better. What's wrong. What? What? It's a
party, isn't it?

*They all watch Hazel get warm. All of them find her attractive. There is a
silence*

Steve I take it all back, Phil.
Phil All of it?
Steve Every last word. Can of beer, Hazel?
Hazel I don't drink.
Steve Pity, you'd have to be careful with this stuff. Knock your bloody head
off.
Hazel Strong is it?
Steve Lethal. Go straight to your legs.
Hazel Very smart, Frank.
Frank Cheers, you don't look too bad yourself.
Phil You're in there, Frankie boy.
Hazel Give it a rest, Phil.
Phil Just a tease, Hazel.
Hazel Just.
Steve You are definitely in tonight.

Hazel Leave it out.

Steve Hazel, you look ravishing. Tell you what, I'll prop, you hook.

Arthur You're not a hooker, are you Hazel?

Hazel No, I'm certainly not.

Frank Shall we get the film on then, or what? I don't want to miss it.

Phil It's a video, Frank, we can put it on when we want.

Frank I know, but you know what I mean?

Phil I wish I did.

Steve (*offering Hazel a low-alcohol beer*) Here you go, Haze, don't say I never do anything for you. It's low-alcohol.

Hazel Cheers, Steve.

Steve You know, I just can't get over it, Hazel.

Hazel What's that?

Steve A wall about thirty feet high with barbed wire and glass at the top. One all. Game on.

Hazel You'll beat me easily, I'm awful with jokes.

Arthur We know that. Come on then. Bring that fire over here, Phil, let's get cosy. Grab a seat, folks, get a good view.

Steve Do you have one in the stalls, Arthur?

Arthur Just down here, Steve.

Steve I want to be near Hazel.

Phil Just put it on if we're going to watch it.

Hazel Better put me somewhere safe, Arthur.

Steve Like at home.

Arthur I wish you lot were half as good on the ball as you are with the bloody wit.

Steve If wit was shit, Phil'd be constipated.

Phil And if you get any thicker Steve, you'll clot.

They all position themselves near to the TV DR. Frank sits to one side of Hazel, Arthur the other. Steve tries to squeeze in but is left at the back. Phil is on the edge of the group

Steve I can't see owt.

Phil Let's watch the test card, it's more interesting.

Frank Come on Arth, you're the projectionist, get it going. All right, Hazel?

Hazel Fine.

Steve That beer cold enough?

Hazel Just right Steve, thanks.

Frank Comfy?

Hazel Yes thanks, Frank.

Frank There's no adverts. That's why I prefer videos. There's no adverts.

Steve There is sometimes, there's Simon Bates. Do you listen to *Our Tune*, Hazel?

Frank I do. It cuts me up. I've written in twice.
Phil Better get the bloody film on before Frank starts weeping all over us.

The overhead lighting goes out; only the glow of the TV screen and the strong warm light from the fire remain

SCENE 3A

The men give a massive childish cheer. Hazel screams

Steve Sorry, sorry — accident.
Hazel You can go off people you know, Steve.
Steve Accident — honest.
Frank Give up messing and watch the film.
Hazel Steve, stop nipping.
Steve Your skin keeps getting caught in my fingers, that's all.
Arthur Steve, pack it in.
Phil It's like being back at bloody school here.
Steve Can I go to the toilet, Mr Hopley, sir?
Phil Yeah, and don't forget to drown yourself.
Steve Go and read a book, Phil.
Phil I wish.
Arthur Pack it in you two, for God's sake; you're so bloody childish.
Phil Look who's talking.
Frank Give it a rest Phil, I can't concentrate.
Phil You don't have to concentrate.
Frank I do.
Arthur Tommy Gunn. That's who he fights.
Steve Boooooo! Hiiissss!
Phil I don't believe I'm actually watching this.
Frank Come on, Rock.
Phil He's not going to lose is he, he can't lose. It's against Hollywood rules.
Frank What's he on about, rules?
Arthur Ignore him Frank, he's a bloody spoilsport.
Phil I'm not.
Hazel Come on Phil, get into it.
Arthur Rocky. Hey Rocky. Rocky Rocky Rocky.

Steve, Frank and Hazel join Arthur in the chant

All Rocky Rocky Rocky Rocky Rocky Rocky.

Black-out

The Lights come up full

All are engrossed in the video. Phil is less happy than the others

Phil Two heavyweights would never last fifteen rounds at that pace, anyway. No way.

Frank I've got some cheese and tomato sandwiches, Phil. Fancy a nibble at that?

Phil I'm too excited to eat, Frank.

Steve Anybody want another can?

Arthur I've had enough.

Steve Not drunk, are you?

Frank It's a film though, innit, it's not real.

Phil Isn't it? I thought it was. Bloody hell.

Steve (*to the video*) Come on the Rock!

Frank D'you fancy a ham sandwich, Hazel? Pig's trotter? A bit of tongue, maybe?

Hazel I never eat after seven, Frank.

Arthur Paulie, Adrienne Brother. (*In a Sylvester Stallone voice*) "Hey Paulie, you bum, hey da Rock."

Steve "Hey Rocky, friends don't owe noth'un."

Arthur "Hey Paulie, friends owe, OK."

Frank Enjoying it, Hazel?

Hazel What, the film or the company?

Phil Don't answer that.

Hazel I like the film. (*She laughs*)

Steve Come on, Phil, "Ain't so bad, ain't so bad."

Phil I should have hung my brain up outside. Then I'd probably enjoy it.

Steve What brain?

Frank Nice one, Steve.

Arthur Do you want to sit here, Hazel? It might be a bit more comfortable.

Frank She's OK here, Arthur.

Arthur She could sit here, it's no problem.

Frank She's OK here.

Arthur Plenty of room here.

Phil She can sit here, I'm going in a minute.

Frank She's all right where she is.

Phil I've got to watch some paint dry.

Hazel I'll sit where I want, OK?

Steve Accident.

Arthur (*annoyed*) Pack it in, Steve, all right?

Hazel There's no need.

Arthur Sorry about this, Hazel.

Hazel Settle him down, Arthur.

Arthur I'll crack him in a minute.

Steve Would I do that on purpose?

Hazel Yes.

Phil Why don't you just watch the video?

Frank We are.

Phil You're not.

Frank I am.

Phil (*referring to Arthur*) Yeah, but *he* isn't.

Arthur I can't watch it because of him.

Hazel I can't sit still because of Steve.

Phil You wanted to watch it, so watch it.

Frank I am watching it.

Steve I've seen it anyway.

Frank We all have.

Phil I haven't.

Steve This is a good bit. Jab him.

Frank Smack him.

Steve Jab and move.

Arthur Jab him.

Frank Smack him.

Hazel Ssh. (*She watches the screen, reacting to the blows*) Ooooh.

Frank Smack him.

Hazel (*grabbing Frank*) Ooooh.

Arthur (*noticing Hazel grabbing Frank*) Come on.

Steve Go for it.

Hazel Urghhhh.

Frank Come on.

Arthur Ummphhhh.

Steve Smack him.

Phil (*exploding*) Kill him for Mickey. Come on Rocky, come on, what're
   you playing at, get up, get up, you're in the street, get up, you silly Italian
   Stallion, get bloody up! Jab and move, jab and then weave, stick him one,
   stick him one, Rock, stick him. Come on, just down him for God's sake,
   then we can all go home!

Black-out

Hazel, Frank and Steve exit; Steve takes the video player with him

SCENE 3C

Much later

The Lights come up. The clubhouse now looks colder. Arthur is obviously feeling rather low. Phil is putting on his coat to leave

Arthur Not such a bad night.

Phil I've had worse.

Arthur Enjoyed it then, did you?

Phil Not exactly *Hamlet*.

Arthur I'm not an academic, Phil, but as far as I can make out the body count in *Hamlet* is pretty high.

Phil That's Art for you.

Arthur I'm not a pig, you know, Phil.

Phil I never said you were.

Arthur And I'm not thick.

Phil Well, given certain evidence that's debatable.

Arthur I know when something's not going right.

Phil What're you on about?

Arthur I mean what is wrong with you; can't you see what you're doing to the team?

Phil I'm not doing anything.

Arthur Aren't you?

Phil No.

Arthur Could've fooled me.

Phil Well, that wouldn't be difficult, would it?

Arthur You're splitting this team right down the middle.

Phil Me?

Arthur That's the way I see it.

Phil It's you.

Arthur What?

Phil If I was you, Arth, I'd concentrate on getting a side together, not the length of Hazel's legs.

Arthur You're talking rubbish, Phil.

Phil So that's why you wanted her to train us in the first place. It's all becoming horribly clear now, Arthur. What's wrong, things not good on the domestic front?

Arthur You're a mile out.

Phil Not jealous of Frank, are you?

Arthur You what?

Phil I saw your face when they left together.

Arthur He's just making sure she gets home all right. We'd all do the same.

Phil Looked a bit serious to me.

Arthur Don't talk such rubbish.

Phil I'm serious.

Arthur You're seeing things, Phil.

Phil Am I?

Arthur Frank can do what he wants. It's none of my business. If him and Hazel are cooking something up between 'em, bully for them. I mean, if they want to carry on like a silly pair of teenagers, big deal. I've got other things to think about. As long as it doesn't interfere with training, fair enough.

Phil Arthur, you're that green with envy, you look like a bloody leprechaun.

Arthur (*suddenly very angry*) Look, forget it, OK, forget it.

Phil Bloody embarrassing, if you ask me.

Arthur Phil, let's leave it, shall we?

Phil I felt like a gooseberry, so God knows how you felt.

Arthur Shut up you stupid get, before I put a soddin' hole in your head.

Phil Oh, right, that's mature.

Arthur I mean it, Phil.

Phil Oh yeah.

Arthur Yeah.

Phil Yeah.

Arthur Yeah.

Phil Yeah.

Arthur I mean it.

Phil Now who's splitting the team?

Arthur Just forget it, all right?

There is a silence

Phil All right, I've forgotten it. Wooosh. Gone out of my mind. Forgotten it forever. I'll never mention it again.

Arthur Right.

Phil Right.

Arthur Thanks.

Phil No problem.

Arthur Great.

There is a pause

Phil But you are jealous, aren't you?

Arthur Course I'm bloody jealous.

Phil Yeah, well, so am I. But let me tell you this, Arthur. I've known Frank a long time, and Tina was never right by him. She led him a right merry jig.

He'd be out training, and she'd be having her own little game back at their
house. Now, all right, what's good for the goose ... and all that, I'm not
taking sides: but if Frank can find a friend in Hazel, whether it lasts or
whether or not it's just a fling, let him enjoy it. I mean he hasn't got a lot
going for him, has he?

Arthur Well, I hate to be contrary, Phil, mate. But it looks to me like our
Frank's got a hell of a lot going for him.

Phil Well, maybe it's about time.

Arthur Yeah, well ...

Phil You know you want to watch that temper, Arthur. You could put people
off their game.

Arthur Too much of what the cat licks its arse with, that's your problem.

Phil And we know what your problem is now, don't we?

Arthur I've got a soft spot for her, that's all.

Phil A crush on her, you mean?

Arthur A crush? I'm thirty-eight, Phil.

Phil Yeah, well ...

Arthur Come on, talk sense. I like her, that's all.

Phil You're like a big kid, Arthur.

Arthur Look, Hazel wouldn't give me a second glance. I mean, look at me.
I'm a wash-out. I'm past it.

Phil Yeah?

Arthur Would she?

Phil (*moving to leave*) Anyway ...

Arthur Would she?

Phil It's academic, isn't it?

Arthur Would she hell.

Phil I don't know, do I?

Arthur So you think she would then, do you?

There is a silence

Phil I'm off.

Phil exits

*Arthur is alone. He picks up an empty beercan. He tries to crush it but he
cannot*

Phil returns

Phil Forgot my fire. (*He unplugs the electric fire and moves to exit*)

Arthur Oh right. Yes. So I'll see you Friday, then, shall I?

Phil If you can get some more players, yeah.

Music plays

The Lights fade to Black-out

SCENE 4

Late afternoon. A few days before Christmas

Outside the clubhouse

The Lights come up. The weather is awful, with rain and thunder. There are several rugby balls on stage

Steve enters with a large umbrella. He has clearly taken it from a beer garden. He is dressed in cagoule and track suit, with neatly gelled hair. He wanders around, testing the ground

Frank enters

Steve The going looks good to soft.
Frank Nice day for ducks.
Steve Quack quack.
Frank Wettest Christmas on record.
Steve Is it?
Frank Do you think we'll have a wet Christmas?
Steve Why not? We've had a wet summer ...
Frank I think we'll have a white Christmas this year.
Steve You could have a white wedding.
Frank What?
Steve Cold, innit?
Frank Somebody's doing something up there, you know? I've never known weather like this. Somebody's interfering with nature.
Steve It's probably Reg Welsh. He's got friends in high places.
Frank Not that high, surely?

There is a pause

Steve D'you get home all right on Wednesday?
Frank Yeah, why?
Steve Nothing, just wondered.
Frank It was a good night. I really enjoyed it. I haven't felt so relaxed in years.

Steve (*misreading*) Oh right.
Frank Hazel came back to our house. I didn't know what to do.
Steve Oh, losing touch, eh?
Frank I didn't know what to talk about.
Steve Where is she?
Frank She's taking one of them step classes. One of the other girls is sick so she's had to step in. I'm picking her up later. I think I'm in there.
Steve I think you are, Frank mate.
Frank Do you think so?
Steve I can't stop long myself. I'm doing our kid's disco while he's away.
Frank We'll not be doing much in this, anyway.
Steve Don't bet on it.
Frank A game of touch and pass and then home.
Steve I'm not running about in this, absolutely no bloody chance. I don't want to get my hair wet. I've got it gelled just right tonight.

Phil enters. He is wearing a cagoule and track suit

Phil Where's all these bloody new recruits then?
Frank Dream on.
Phil I'm giving it ten minutes and then I'm off. Null and void, forget it.
Frank Where's Arthur?
Steve His car's here.
Phil Ten minutes.
Frank We must be crackers.
Phil (*referring to the umbrella*) This is good, Steve.
Steve It's from the *Wheatsheaf*. I'm getting my own back on Stan. I'm keeping it.
Frank I think it's easing off.
Steve Where?

Arthur enters. He is wearing a cagoule and carrying a bag, a street cone and a very large rubber inner tube

Arthur Wonderful. You look a bloody picture.
Steve You're not coming under our brolly. You should have brought one of your own.

During the following, Arthur works his way under the umbrella

Arthur Fog and mist forecast.
Phil Ay, and a plague of frogs and all.
Arthur Look, let's get sommat done.

Phil Where's all the recruits, Arthur?

Arthur Can we get sommat sorted, and then play it by ear?

Steve Play rugby by ear? That'd be novel.

Arthur Let's just think about the game.

Phil Ten minutes.

Arthur I want to do some shuttle runs, work on a new move — and I want
    to see Steve do some tackling.

Steve Wash your mouth out.

Arthur OK? We'll give it fifteen minutes and then home?

Phil Ten.

Arthur Come on, then, let's get out there.

Steve Go on, then.

Arthur Eh?

Steve Let's see you get out there.

Arthur I've just been out there.

Steve Well, go out there again, then.

Frank It's like a bloody monsoon now.

Arthur Right, I'll count to three, and then we'll all run out, right? Ready.

Steve
Phil } (*together*) Ay. Right. Go on then.
Frank

Arthur One. Two. Three.

Arthur runs from under the umbrella. The other three remain where they are.
Arthur places the cone DC *and runs back under the umbrella*

  Bloody hell, lads.

Frank What's it like?

Arthur What're you playing at?

Phil I can't swim, Arthur.

Arthur You'll get used to it.

Steve I've got used to this.

Phil Oh look, Arthur, you're dripping all over me.

Arthur I'm not.

Phil You are.

Arthur Right, come on this time. A few shuttle runs to get us warm. It's from
    the brolly, around the skittle and back under the brolly. Right.

Steve Ay, come on.

Frank Watch it, though, it could be slippery.

Phil Ay, it could be, Frank, you're right there. Be careful, Arthur, we've had
    ten inches of rain in the last two hours so it might be a bit slippery.

Steve Take a funny pill, Phil.

Arthur Go.

Arthur sets off from under the umbrella. He rounds the cone and runs back under the umbrella. On his return, Frank sets out on the same course

Phil Careful, Frank, it could be slippery.

As Frank returns to the umbrella Phil sets out, shouting "Go" to himself. He makes a quick circuit around the cone and then goes back under the umbrella

Arthur Come on, you Water Babies.

They are all now under the umbrella. It is Steve's turn to run

Arthur Steve, go ...
Phil Go, Stevie-boy ...

Steve sets off on his run, but he takes the umbrella with him, snaking around the stage with the others following after him. He finds this very funny. Finally, on another part of the stage, the others catch up with him. He is in fits. The others are less happy about it

Arthur Very funny.
Phil Nice one, Steve.
Steve It got you warm, didn't it?
Arthur Right Steve, let's have a look at your tackling.
Frank Why? He never does any.
Arthur Frank, can you not be so negative? I mean I don't know what's got into you, but you're very negative.
Frank I'm not.
Arthur Just bring us that inner tube, will you?

Frank collects the inner tube, brings it to Arthur and then shelters in the lee of the clubhouse. Phil and Steve are still under the umbrella. Arthur moves downstage with the inner tube and demonstrates what he wants Steve to do with it

Arthur Right, this is a member of the opposition. A *Cobblers* centre.
Frank Looks like an inner tube to me.
Arthur Use your imagination, Frank, it's a wonderful thing. I want to see you dipping your shoulder, Steve, and put in a low tackle.
Steve I'm doing a disco tonight, you know.
Arthur So what.
Steve I don't want to get mucky.
Frank Not yet, anyway.

Phil Not till after midnight.

Frank If he's lucky.

Arthur Come on, Steve, bloody hell. Low and hard. Let's see a bit of action. I'm sodden.

Steve All right, keep your hair on, but I'm only doing it once.

Phil That's all you do in a game, anyway.

Steve Get ready then, Arthur. I'm coming for you.

Arthur Come on, Steve, show us what you're made of.

Steve runs DS. *Arthur rolls the inner tube towards Steve, who flails at it in a rather pathetic way and falls with it to the ground*

Phil Nice tackle.

Arthur They've scored, Steve. They're through and scored. They've scored and we've lost.

Frank He couldn't stop a cheque.

Steve Look at my bloody hair. I'm soaked.

Arthur Not bad, Steve lad, not bad. Least you had a go.

Steve sits in the inner tube as if it is a small sailing dinghy

Frank I don't think anybody's going to show.

Steve I'm gunna have to get off home, Arth — I mean, look at me. This isn't even my cagoule, I nicked it from the *Wheatsheaf.*

Frank It's a wash-out, this.

Phil Brilliant.

Steve I'm gunna get pneumonia if I stay out here much longer.

Frank Come under here, then.

Steve Too late. I'm bloody drenched now, aren't I, you silly get.

Frank Hey, steady on ...

Steve Look at me bloody hair.

Frank Just don't call me a silly get, all right?

Phil That's it, Arth. I'm off, mate.

Arthur What about working a few half-back moves, Phil? Let's work a few half-back moves.

Phil Up my arse, Arthur, all right?

Frank Don't call me a silly get.

Steve Well you are, Frank. We all are.

There is a silence

Arthur Right then, let's have a quick game of unopposed rugby.

Steve Forget it.

Arthur Twice round the field and then home, eh?
Frank Let's get in the *'Sheaf* and have a bloody skinful.
Steve That's a better idea.
Arthur So that's it then, is it?
Phil It's over, Arthur.
Frank It's finished.
Steve Look at my bloody hair.
Frank Looks better, if you ask me.

There is a silence

Arthur (*with difficulty*) That's it, lads. That's enough. I'm saturated. It's finished. Let's get off bloody home, get in the *Wheatsheaf* and get utterly legless.
Phil You lads go, I'm off home.

There is a lightning flash and a roll of thunder. Music plays as the men prepare to leave, zipping up their cagoules and picking up the rugby balls

Spud enters. He is a young giant, very West Yorkshire, with a naïve attitude and a slightly slow response rate. The rain doesn't seem to bother him

Spud *Wheatsheaf Arms*?
Arthur Ar, we're just finishing, cock. You've missed us.
Spud Rugby training?
Phil It was.
Spud Heard it on t'radio other day. I was up messin' wi' mi' CB in t'loft, when it broke through.
Steve One-nine for a copy.
Frank He's had some meat pies, a'n't he, Arthur?
Spud It said sommat about you looking for players. Well, there's nowt on t' telly so I thought I'd turn out.
Arthur Oh, right.
Spud I'm Spud.
Steve Ten Roge Spud, I'm Steve.
Arthur This is Phil, Frank; I'm Arthur.
Spud Are we training then or what?
Arthur Listen, Spud, we were just calling it a day, you know with the weather and that. Fog forecast.
Spud It'll not bother me. You can only get wet once, can't you?
Steve I don't know about that.
Arthur Well I don't suppose another half hour will hurt, will it, Phil?

There is a pause

Phil No, no, I suppose not.

Arthur Phil's one of our top players. A brilliant half-back.

Phil (*falsely modest*) Well, I wouldn't go that far.

Arthur Have you played much rugby lately?

Spud Not lately.

Arthur Have you played anything lately?

Spud No.

Arthur Have you done owt lately?

Spud I've learnt bass guitar.

Steve Have you heard that new Meatloaf album?

Phil Have a minute, Steve. Don't be stupid.

Steve There's a good bass line on it.

Phil When was the last time you handled a ball?

Spud I played in York about two years ago.

Phil St John's?

Spud St John's, yeah, it wa'.

Phil What about fitness?

Spud What about it?

Frank Can you do ten press-ups?

Spud Ten. Can you?

Frank I can do eight.

Steve Eight, is that all? I can do seven.

Arthur All right then, Spud, let's see what you're like with a ball. I'll spin a few out to you, let's see what you're like.

Arthur throws a ball to Spud. Spud cannot make contact with the ball. It slips away from him and is retrieved by Phil

Phil Very good. How long have we got?

Spud I wasn't ready.

Phil No, that's right.

Spud Ball's a bit slippery, that's all.

Arthur Yeah, not bad, Spud.

Spud Like I said, it's been a couple of years.

Arthur Yeah. Not bad at all, that, cock. But you see we've had a big response, you know, and there's a lot of lads to pick from. And, well, we play on Boxing Day and there's not a lot of time to get you into shape.

Spud I'm keen.

Phil And that's about all.

Spud You what?

Phil You're never going to get there, are you?

Arthur I don't think it's going to work, sunshine.

Spud Just spin another pass to me, just try me with another.

There is a pause

Phil No, come on, let's leave it.
Arthur Let's call that it, shall we?
Spud All I'm asking for is a chance.
Frank Give him a bloody chance.
Phil He's had a chance, Frank, come on, can't you see? He's useless. No
  offence, mate. But I mean he's not experienced enough.
Frank Pity. He's big enough.
Steve He's like an house side.
Spud Well, I walked all the way down here; I thought I'd at least get a game.
Arthur Look, I tell you what. We need a bucket man; why don't you come
  and carry the water bucket. Cut the oranges up, wash the kit, eh?
Spud I want to play.
Arthur Not with us, kid.
Spud Be fair.
Arthur I am being.
Spud Hey look, I know I don't look like I'm any good. But I can play, you
  know. I played two games at York, second row. Just spin another one to
  me.
Steve I'm going to have to leg it, Arth. I'm soaked through to my skin.
Phil Look, don't call us, we'll call you, all right?
Steve I'll have to get changed. I can't run a disco like this, I'll electrocute
  myself.
Frank (*to Spud*) Come and carry the bucket, eh, help us out?
Arthur That's the best I can offer you, Spud, a place on the touchline.
Spud Be right ...
Arthur Sorry, bud.
Spud Oh, what ... ?
Arthur Sorry.
Spud Well, I was trying to do you a good turn and all. I tell you this much—
  I hope you get bloody thrashed. Carry the bucket — you must think I'm
  off mi perch.

*Spud exits. The others remain, looking cold and damp. Music plays. Then
there is silence*

Frank Poor sod. He's dying for a game.
Steve Do you know him?
Phil He can only just string a sentence together.
Arthur I feel awful for turning him away, but what could we do with him?
  We haven't got time to be starting from scratch with somebody.
Frank How's he gunna get back?

Steve He'll probably nick a car.

Arthur Well I hope he doesn't nick mine.

Phil He's obviously not carrying a full load, is he? Who'd turn out in this
   weather?

Frank Well ——

Phil Don't answer that, Frank.

Arthur But he turned up, Phil.

Phil He did that.

Arthur He turned up, and you said if somebody turned up you'd still play.

Phil Hang on.

Steve Yes, you bloody did.

Phil Wait a minute.

Arthur Yes, you bloody did.

Frank Good old Spud.

Phil No, hang on ——

Arthur Three cheers for Spud.

Phil No.

Arthur Yes. Hip hip hooray. Hip hip hooray.

*Phil doesn't join in the celebrations. Arthur, Steve and Frank cheer and
laugh at Phil*

   *The atmosphere is broken by the arrival of Doreen. She is a plain woman
   in her mid-thirties wearing a raincoat. She looks like she's been very upset*

Doreen Oh, right. She said you'd be here.

Arthur Doreen.

Doreen Can we have a word?

Arthur Just finishing, love.

Doreen Either here or at the pub, she said.

Arthur Just about done.

Doreen I've been down to the gym. Very smart.

Phil Aren't you going to introduce us, Arthur?

Doreen She seems very nice.

Arthur (*eager to see the back of the team*) Right lads, that's enough for one
   night. Well done, everybody. Good work. Thanks a lot.

Phil Sure you don't want us to do a bit more, Arthur?

Arthur No, that's enough for one night, Phil.

Phil I'm hardly sweating, we could have another half hour if you wanted. I'm
   in for that.

Frank Good idea, that. I'll have a game of touch and pass.

Steve D'you fancy a game, Mrs Hoyle?

Arthur Good lads, these, Doreen. Obsessed with the game, this lot. (*To the
   lads*) No, you lot, get off. I'll see to everything.

Doreen Working you hard, is he?

Steve We can't get enough of it, eh, Arth?

Arthur That's right.

Doreen Can we have a chat?

Arthur Course.

Doreen In private.

Phil Well, we'd better get off, Arthur. See you for a skinful in the *'Sheaf.* I'll put you a pint in the bin.

Steve Ay, it might taste a lot better.

Frank Nice to meet you. Don't be too hard on him, it's not worth it.

Doreen Don't worry. I won't.

Arthur She loves me to death. (*To Doreen*) Don't you?

Phil, Steve and Frank exit. The atmosphere between Arthur and Doreen is very icy

Arthur What're you doing up here? You'll catch your death.

Doreen Looking for you.

Arthur In this weather?

Doreen I've had enough ...

Arthur Why, what's up, what's happened?.

Doreen I've really had enough of it this time.

Arthur Well, tell me what's happened; is it your Mam? Is she bad again?

Doreen Bloody Christmas and you have to be doing this.

Arthur I've finished now. I was just on my way home.

Doreen I just don't believe it.

Arthur Don't go on, I've said I've finished.

Doreen You're a worm, Arthur.

Arthur What ... ?

Doreen You are ——

Arthur What, what what have I done now?

Doreen What?

Arthur Yeah.

Doreen My dad heard you on the radio.

A beat

Arthur Oh right.

Doreen Yeah.

A beat

Arthur I just ... I didn't ——

Doreen Why did you lie to me?

Arthur Let's go home and talk about this, can we ... ?

Doreen Why didn't you tell me?

Arthur What would you have said?

Doreen Why didn't you tell me?

Arthur I couldn't. I was going to, but I couldn't. What would you have said?

Doreen Six thousand pounds.

Arthur I know ...

Doreen Six thousand pounds.

Arthur There's no need to cause an upset.

Doreen No need to cause an upset?

Arthur We'll win.

Doreen (*getting emotional*) You're causing the upset.

Arthur I swear we'll win.

Doreen We haven't got that sort of cash.

Arthur I know.

Doreen I've got nothing in my purse. Do you want to see? Look look, nothing in my purse. (*She opens her purse and forces Arthur to look inside it*) I could kill you, I could, I could slit your bloody throat. I mean, I just do not believe it. We've got no work lined up in the New Year. The order book's bloody empty, nobody wants our business because of the fool you made of yourself last time. We're a laughing stock, but it doesn't matter. I'll just do what I want. Arthur, you open your mouth and rubbish comes out ...

Arthur Doreen, listen ...

Doreen How could you do it?

Arthur I don't know.

Doreen (*very emotional*) How could you do it to us?

Arthur Listen to me.

Doreen No.

Arthur Listen to me.

Doreen I don't want to listen, I can't believe a word you say.

Arthur I didn't want to hurt you, that's why I didn't tell you.

Doreen I want you to make your mind up.

Arthur Don't do this to me.

Doreen I want you to decide what it is you want. Because I'll tell you this. If you go through with this game I don't want you to come home.

Arthur Come on, love ...

Doreen Don't "love" me ...

Arthur Love ...

Doreen I said don't ...

Arthur Wonderful. That's very helpful, thanks.

Doreen Cancel the game.

There is a silence

Arthur How can I cancel the game?
Doreen That's what I want you to do. Then we can get our lives back together.
Arthur What do you mean, get our lives back together? It's just a game of rugby, for God's sake.
Doreen Is it?
Arthur Please listen to me.
Doreen And when you've decided what to do about the game, we'll be able to talk about you and her.
Arthur Who?
Doreen Arthur, I wasn't born yesterday.
Arthur She's just helping with the team.
Doreen So what're you going to do ... ?

There is a silence

Arthur I can't cancel the game.
Doreen Are you coming back or are you staying here?
Arthur I need you.

There is a pause

Doreen So you're going through with it?
Arthur What can I say ... ?
Doreen How about sorry?
Arthur You know I love you, love ...
Doreen Do I?

Doreen exits

In the distance Christmas carols can be heard; snow falls. Arthur is cold, distraught and alone

Doreen enters. She is carrying a number of cases and plastic bags and some of Arthur's videos. She throws everything on to the floor

Doreen I've changed the locks. If you change your mind, ring me.
Arthur Doreen.
Doreen You'd better think about it. Because I'm serious.
Arthur What can I do?

Doreen walks away, then stops and turns to Arthur

Doreen Your presents are in the carrier.
Arthur Please, love ...

Silence

Doreen Oh, by the way — Merry Christmas.

She exits

Arthur slowly rises, collects his baggage and exits in the opposite direction to that taken by Doreen

Music

The Lights fade to Black-out

CURTAIN

ACT II

SCENE 1

Outside the clubhouse. December 23rd. Early evening

The Lights come up. It is very crisp and cold

Hazel, Phil, Steve and Arthur are training; all are wrapped up against the severe weather. They are doing sit-ups in pairs. Phil and Steve are one pair, with Phil holding Steve's feet, Hazel and Arthur are the other. Phil's sports bag is US; rugby balls lie around

Ray Mason enters from the clubhouse

Steve No more.
Phil Come on ...
Hazel Push it, Arthur ...
Arthur I am.
Ray (*turning on his tape recorder and beginning to commentate*)This is Ray Mason, this is "Sports Scene", and this is a "Sports Scene Special".
Hazel Push it, Steve ...
Ray With only two days to go before the big game, there are only forty-eight hours of waiting left to wait.
Hazel (*shouting*) Work it ...
Steve I am.
Arthur Shout at me.
Hazel (*shouting*) Come on.
Ray Things are certainly hotting up here. I'm concentrating on the game so much that I don't know what I'm thinking about half the time ——
Hazel Another.
Ray —— in fact all the time.
Hazel Push it, you two, push it.
Arthur Ahhhhhh, that's it ...

Arthur and Steve stop doing their sit-ups. They stand and try to keep warm

Ray While the *Cobblers* train at their luxury hideaway in Rothwell, the *Wheatsheaf Arms* are braving it out on Walton Fields, and it's bitterly cold here. Some say it's the coldest winter on record ——

Steve It bloody is.

Ray — and I would tend to agree with them. There's even ice on the ball. Arthur Hoyle is with me. How are things looking, Arthur?

Arthur Not too bad, Ray.

Ray Not long to go: what would you say the odds are?

Arthur Stacked, Ray.

Ray And no luck with new players?

Arthur Not a lot.

Ray I'm joined now by other members of the *Wheatsheaf* team. So, what do you think about the game?

Steve I think we should cancel it and play it next summer.

Ray Why's that?

Steve I'm emigrating.

Arthur Come off the mike, Steve ...

Steve He asked me.

Phil You're stupid.

Steve I am, you're right there.

Ray Hazel, you're training the team. It must be great fun working with all these butch men.

Hazel Are you serious?

Arthur (*coming to the mike in Hazel's defence*) Hazel's doing a great job, actually. And I think there's a lot of teams who'd benefit from a female instructor.

Phil Creep.

Ray Arthur, I understand that the team has been plagued with a number of minor thefts this week?

Arthur That's right, Ray. Steve's had some records stolen, Phil's car's been broken into. And I've had five tins of paint that've gone missing.

Ray And this the season of goodwill?

Arthur Let's just say we've got a pretty good idea where all this is coming from.

Phil But we can't prove it.

Ray You will, of course, be aware by now of the inclusion of Big Jim Stone in the *Cobblers* side.

Steve What?

Arthur No comment.

Steve You're joking.

Ray Big Jim is, of course, an ex-*Cobbler* Amateur and retired Great Britain International.

Steve The man's a maniac.

Ray How do you feel about that?

Arthur No comment.

Steve Jim Stone, Jim Stone: that is it, that is it. We are all dead.

Ray Last time, of course, you had a secret weapon with Hazel. Any similar plans this time?

Spud enters, wearing an old and tatty track suit and duffel coat. He is carrying a bucket

Spud Bet you thought you'd never see me again, eh?
Arthur Oh, bloody hell.
Steve He can take my place.
Spud Come on, spin one to me, spin me one. Pass, mate. Come, bud, pass.
Phil (*holding the ball*) No.
Spud Oh, stick it, then.
Ray Well, we've just been joined by another member of the *Wheatsheaf* team.
Arthur Hang on ...
Ray A second row forward, if I've ever seen one.
Arthur Hold on, Ray, he's just hanging about.
Spud Hey, I've even brought me own bucket. Good laugh, eh? (*To Phil*) Come on, spin me one.
Phil No.
Arthur He's not on the side.
Spud Thought I'd come and give you a second chance.
Ray What do you think the outcome of the game will be? Do the *Wheatsheaf* have a hope in hell?
Spud Who, this lot? No chance, not unless they let me play. Tell you sommat, they ought to get me on for 'em. Put me in at scrum half; I'll use my size. Or on the wing. Play me anywhere, Boss, just play me.
Ray Do you think it'll be an open game?
Spud I think they've got to hit 'em — flat, blanket defence. Man and ball.
Ray Is there anything you'd like to say to the *Cobblers*?
Spud Yeah, are my shoes ready yet? Smart laugh. Hear that. (*He grabs the mike*) Hey, one-nine for a copy, pick a lucky window, you've got the Elephant Man. Good buddy, I'm up in that Fish City just north of the knowledge college ... Is that a Roge?... Ten-four ... Hey, good bud, looks like we've got ourselves a convoy ——
Ray (*furious*) Come here, get off that ...
Spud Smart laugh.
Ray Are you completely thick? Just pack it in.
Spud Steady on.
Ray You dozy sod.
Spud You what?
Ray This is expensive.
Spud I'm only having a mess about.

Arthur Come on, Spud, just go away, all right?

Spud I tell thee sommat: don't talk to me like that or I'll punch a hole in thee neck.

Ray Oh really?

Spud Yeah. Oh really.

Hazel Arthur, do you think we can possibly push on?

Arthur Look, go and stand over there with your bucket.

Spud Bloody media.

Steve Come over here, Spud.

Spud (*moving over to Steve*) I bet they edit it to make me look bad.

Hazel (*slightly put out*) Are we getting on or shall I go home?

Ray It's volatile, it's aggressive, there's a real sense of anarchy about it, but this is the way the *Wheatsheaf* train. They're sending a message out to the *Cobblers*: "Look out, these men are dangerous." (*He turns off his recorder*) That's good radio, Arthur. Lovely. All the heat of the battle. Thanks very much, everyone. I don't know when it'll go out, but all the best for the match. See you on the day.

Ray exits

Steve If you're lucky.

Hazel Shall we get on?

Steve Look, I'm gunna have to get off. I've got another booking for "Midnight Blue".

Phil "Midnight Blue"?

Steve Our young 'un's disco. I'm doing the *Earl De Grey* and a fancy dress up at Willerby. From the sublime to the ridiculous. I think I've found my vocation.

Phil Fancy dress? Are we invited?

Steve No, I didn't invite you, Phil. I thought you'd be spending the night with Zola or whoever she is. You can come if you want. Hazel?

Hazel No, thanks.

Arthur We've only got one more training session after this, Steve.

Steve Yeah, but I don't want to over-train. I'm at my peak. So I won't be there on Wednesday. I'm ready, don't worry. Listen, I'll be there on the day.

Arthur Don't let me down, Steve ...

Steve exits

There is a silence. They all want to leave

Hazel So I suppose that's it for today, then, is it? Another pathetic training session.

Arthur Yes, Hazel, pathetic and fractured, but that is it. Another session over. Well, I'm sorry if we aren't the bloody A team. (*Pause*) Sorry. I just didn't have such a good night's sleep last night ... I ... Sorry.

Phil Arthur, can I have a quickie?

Arthur Why, can't you make it for training either? What a surprise.

Phil I just thought that Spud might be just what we're looking for.

Spud No chance, I'm not playing, I'm only here to carry the bucket. No, I'm only joking. Go on, gi's a game.

Phil Fancy a game, eh, Spud?

Spud (*referring to Hazel*) Is she on the team?

Phil Yes.

Spud Smart laugh.

Phil I thought we could move the ball about a bit, you know, have a game of unopposed.

Hazel That's kids' stuff.

Phil Exactly.

Spud Unopposed?

Arthur Let's just waste as much time as we possibly can, OK? Let's just waste time.

Phil We'll just start slowly, build up a bit of confidence and see what your positional play is like.

Spud Gi's a touch of the ball.

Phil In a minute.

Arthur Let's leave it, Phil.

Hazel I think we should push on.

Phil No, hang on. Right, Spud. We're going to imagine that we're playing against the *Cobblers*.

Spud (*looking at the imaginary* Cobblers) Big, aren't they?

Hazel Massive.

Phil I call "Tackle", the man tackled plays the ball, and we realign for the next attack, right?

Spud Easy stuff.

Phil Arthur, you have the ball. (*He throws the ball to Arthur*)

Arthur Very educational. (*He falls to the floor*)

Phil Right, stand by for a ball on the run, Spud.

Hazel comes as First Receiver. She passes to Phil, Phil looks to pass to Spud, but ...

"Tackle." Play the ball, stand by Spud, Hazel in at half-back, Spud nice and deep ...

Spud (*speaking to the imaginary* Cobblers) Oh yeah, call that a tackle, it was up around his neck, man. It was a mile too high.

Phil Spud, your ball.

Spud Oh yeah, we'll see about that, mate. You passing the hospital? You will be. Nearly took his head off.

Arthur What?

Phil Your ball, Spud ...

Spud See that ... You all right, Arthur?

Arthur Eh?

Phil What?

Spud High tackle, stiff arm, they ought to ban him.

Arthur Oh, bloody hell.

Spud Ref ... ref ... are you blind?

Hazel Spud, wait a minute ...

Spud Get him off, man ...

Phil Wow, steady ...

Spud Get him sent off — off — off !(*He cackles*) Brilliant, smart laugh. Good game, innit? High tackle, excellent. Hey Arthur, unopposed rugby and we still didn't score. Bit sad that?

Phil What's going on?

Spud Well, tha said imagine.

Phil I did. I did, yes.

Spud Smart. I knew as soon as you said it, I'd get you. Smart laugh. Come on again, I'll do it right this time.

Arthur No.

Spud Hey, come on, be right, he said imagine.

The ring of a mobile phone can be heard; it is coming from Phil's sports bag. This throws Phil into a panic; he runs to answer the phone

Arthur Ay, he did, yeah. Listen, imagine we're not playing, all right. I'll train the team, play the game, wash the shirts and carry the bloody bucket. Right? Right. We don't want you.

Spud Come on, I was only having a mess ... What's up, can't you take a joke?

Arthur No.

Hazel Look, it's just getting a bit tense, that's all.

Spud Tense. It will be in a minute.

Phil (*into the phone*) Yes. ... OK. Yes, yes. ... OK, Molly, yes. ... OK, don't panic. I'm coming. ... Yes. Don't panic. (*He puts the phone down*) Arthur, I ... er ... She's started. I'm away. Sorry. But. Well, anyway. All the best. I'll be there if I can. Hazel, sorry.

Hazel Go, Phil.

Phil It's Carol ... you know ... she's ...

Hazel Go ...

Phil If I can't make the game, all the best. Play it wide, OK? Swing it out.

Arthur Swing it out ... who to ...?
Hazel Philip, just go — now.
Phil Thanks.
Hazel You're dismissed.
Phil Oh, I'm going to be a dad, I can't believe it.

Phil exits, leaving his bag and phone

Spud (*picking up Phil's bag quite naturally*) I'll get off and all then, shall I?
Arthur Would you?
Spud Training tomorrow?
Arthur It's Christmas Eve.
Spud When are you training again, then?
Arthur Next March.
Spud Oh ar.
Arthur Christmas Day.
Spud Christmas Day. I'll bring some cake.
Arthur Night.
Spud I'll be there.
Arthur Do you have to ... ?
Spud Hey up.
Hazel Look, Spud, I think it'd be better if you didn't.
Arthur (*defeated*) Oh leave him, Hazel, let him come if he wants.
Spud Smart laugh. I'll get off, then. Might get on t' bass tonight, annoy my neighbours.

Spud exits, taking Phil's phone and bag with him

There is a silence

Hazel Shall we call that it?
Arthur Can do.
Hazel Do you fancy a pint in the *'Sheaf*? I'll join you if you want.
Arthur No thanks. I'm staying here.
Hazel You can't stay here.
Arthur I did last night. Frozen to death, I was.
Hazel What's happened?
Arthur Don't ask.
Hazel Are you OK? You're not, are you?
Arthur I'm in a bit of a state at the moment.
Hazel What do you mean?
Arthur I mean emotionally.
Hazel Is it the game?

Arthur Well ... yes ... and no.

Hazel What is it?

Arthur Ar ... it's ... Well ...

Hazel Can I help? I mean, is it something you can talk about? I mean, do you want to ... Sorry. Is it personal or what?

Arthur (*carefully*) Well the thing is ... I've got these feelings. And I haven't had feelings like this for years. I mean, I feel about thirteen. And. Well. I know it's stupid. I mean, I laid there all night telling myself it's stupid but the feelings won't go away. And I don't know what to do about it ...

Hazel Yeah?

Arthur Yeah ...

Hazel You know, I know it might sound strange, but I feel a bit like that at the moment.

Arthur Yeah?

Hazel I feel like I'm a bag of emotions.

Arthur Wearing your heart on your sleeve?

Hazel Yeah, yeah.

Arthur I know what you mean.

Hazel And we're supposed to be adults?

Arthur Insane, isn't it?

Hazel Madness.

Arthur Funny thing is, Hazel, I knew I'd be able to open up to you.

Hazel I feel the same with you.

Arthur No?

Hazel I do.

Arthur You're joking?

Hazel I'm not. It's just that we never really get time to talk.

Arthur Well ... we're talking now. At last.

Hazel I've felt on edge since last Wednesday.

Arthur I thought it was weird when you just went.

Hazel I knew you'd be offended. But it won't work out, you know.

Arthur It might.

Hazel No.

Arthur Give it a chance.

Hazel I have.

Arthur You haven't.

Hazel I have, believe me ——

Arthur Yeah, but ——

Hazel Frank's a good bloke, you know——

Arthur Frank? I thought ——

Hazel He's really smashing ——

Arthur I thought ——

Hazel I don't want either of us to get hurt ——

Arthur No, no.
Hazel But I don't know what to do.
Arthur Yeah, yeah?
Hazel He's supposed to be stuffing a turkey for me tonight.
Arthur Lucky him.
Hazel Hey, I nearly forgot. I — er — couldn't think of anything to get you.

Hazel gives Arthur a wrapped-up video from her bag

Arthur What is it?
Hazel Guess.
Arthur "A Hundred and One Top Rugby League Tries".
Hazel No.
Arthur Oh. (*He unwraps the present. It is "A Hundred and One Top Rugby League Tries"*) "A Hundred and One Top Rugby League Tries". Great. Just what I wanted.
Hazel You haven't got it, have you?
Arthur No, no ...
Hazel Have you?
Arthur Well another one's always handy, isn't it?
Hazel I thought it might inspire you.
Arthur Thanks a lot, Hazel.
Hazel It's the thought that counts.
Arthur Yeah.
Hazel Anyway.
Arthur You'd better go.
Hazel Yeah.

Hazel exits

Arthur is sad and alone

Arthur Frank'll be waiting for you.

The Lights fade to Black-out

Music

SCENE 2

The interior of Reg's house. Christmas Day

Reg's house is opulent, expensive and beautiful, in sharp contrast to anything we have seen so far. A large trophy dominates the room

The Lights come up. Reg, dressed smartly in shirt, tie and jumper, sits with Ray, drinking champagne. They chink their glasses

Both Cheers.

Ray All the best, Reg.

Reg And may the best team win.

Ray Absolutely.

Reg Well, there it is, Ray. The Reg Welsh Trophy. That's a symbol of the importance I attach to the amateur game. Worth two grand of anybody's money, that is.

Ray A lovely piece of work, Reg.

Reg So you reckon they look useful, do you?

Ray It's difficult to tell, Reg. He seems to be putting 'em through it. They must be as hard as nails. I mean, he's ignoring all the modern training methods.

Reg He wants flat caps and whippets on the touchline. Suffocating change. How're we going to compete on the playing fields of Eton with blokes like Arthur in the game? It's bad enough convincing that lot down south that we play the better code, without having clowns like him. One day I went to sit and watch England play Wales at Twickenham and there be nobody in the crowd, they're all at Craven Park watching Fulham. The ratings game, that's what we're in now. And I want some of these working-class lads to show some respect. Because it doesn't come easy, Ray. Star quality doesn't come easy.

Ray He adds a bit of colour though, Reg.

Reg Training in weather like this? Bloody barmy. Why doesn't he concede? I'll let him off with half the cash. He's not using drugs, is he?

Ray He must be using something, Reg, and that's for sure.

Reg By the way, Ray, there's a small token of my gratitude in the post for you.

Ray Most generous. Lovely.

Reg Just a little "Thank you".

Ray Who's reffing, do you know?

Reg Colin West.

Ray From Hemsworth?

Reg We were in the Youth Squad together. A good ref is Colin. Stands no nonsense. Any back chat and it's the Sin Bin.

Ray I noticed you'd put an advert in the "Mail". So there might be a decent turnout.

Reg And I've invited the Mayor. A big fan.

Ray I know.

Reg A big fan.

Ray Lovely bloke.

Reg Besides they've put some double yellow lines outside my club. I want to have a word about it. Can't park outside my own club.

Ray Wicked.

Reg Then there's the warehouse development I need to chat about.

Ray Good for the city.

Reg And some office space I want to get rid of.

Ray Recession?

Reg Bloody nuisance. A rag bag team, this lot, Ray. Couldn't run a raffle.

Ray Will there be a raffle?

Reg We could arrange one. First prize: Arthur's teeth.

Ray I'm trying to cover the match with an OB.

Reg Make sure you do. I want maximum publicity.

Ray Lovely drop of bubbly, Reg.

Reg A drop more?

Ray Wouldn't say no ...

More champagne is poured

Reg Yes ... I want to see that toe-rag totally humiliated this time. You know that I used to court his missus?

Ray I didn't.

Reg Years back this is. Childhood sweethearts we were, me and Doreen. Nice woman. What she ever saw in him I'll never know.

Ray You don't still fancy her, then ... ?

Reg She's a lovely woman. Anyway, Ray, me and Vicky are settled. We've had our ups and downs, and who hasn't? She's in Marbella at the moment, sunning herself. I'm joining her in the New Year.

Ray So it is personal, then?

Reg Everything's personal, Ray.

Pause

In Amateur Rugby League, everything is personal.

Music plays

The Lights fade to Black-out

SCENE 3

Outside the clubhouse. Christmas Day. Night

*The Lights come up. It is crisp and cold. Arthur is on stage, wrapped against
the cold and removing the ice from a rugby ball with a windscreen scraper
and a can of de-icer spray*

Arthur Bloody ice.

*Spud enters. He too is wrapped against the cold in an old duffel coat. He
carries a plastic bag and wears fingerless gloves*

Spud Where are they?
Arthur Good question.
Spud Legged it?
Arthur They'll be here.
Spud Are we training then, or what?
Arthur Me and you? Who will we pass to?
Spud We could do some kicking.
Arthur In this light?
Spud I've already thought about that.

Spud brings a luminous rugby ball out of his bag. It glows

Arthur Bloody hell.
Spud Spot the ball. Eh, I could patent this. Save electric. Think of that, eh,
  green rugby? I could make a fortune.
Arthur Dunno.
Spud Shall we do some kicking? You need a good kicker, don't you?
Arthur How do you know?
Spud I saw the last game. Anyway, I've brought these. Cold on your feet but
  good for practice.

*Spud brings a pair of old slippers out of his bag and puts them on during the
following dialogue*

Arthur Slippers?
Spud Ay, its the Neil Fox theory: if you can kick in slippers, you can kick
  in anything.
Arthur So they reckon.
Spud These aren't mine, they're my aunty's.
Arthur She a big woman?

Spud Yeah, I'm the smallest in our family.
Arthur I suppose you don't have much trouble with the rent man?
Spud Not a lot. Right. Here we go. (*He is ready to practise*) Maybe we should paint the posts?
Arthur I was just thinking, I had some luminous paint.
Spud Yeah?
Arthur Somebody took off with it.
Spud Can't trust anybody these days. Hold the ball.

Arthur holds the ball upright DS. *Spud moves backwards, preparing to run forward and kick the ball*

Arthur Why am I doing this? Just watch my fingers.
Spud Oh, hell.
Arthur What's wrong?
Spud I think I've stood in sommat.
Arthur What?
Spud Has there been some dogs up here?
Arthur Might have.
Spud Oh, what ... ?
Arthur Come on ...
Spud It's all over my slippers.
Arthur I'm freezing here.
Spud My aunty'll kill me. Hang on a bit, let's get this off. (*He wipes the slippers clean*)

Frank enters with his bag, very dejected. He doesn't look as if he wants to train

Frank All right?
Arthur Late, aren't you?
Frank Sorry.
Arthur Where've you been? You look frozen.
Frank Just drifting.
Arthur Drifting?
Frank Stayed in all day, didn't go to see the kids, and then I decided to drift up here.
Arthur That's big of you. What happened to the turkey feast?
Frank That was yesterday.
Arthur Thought you and Hazel were having a romantic night?
Frank We were. (*He produces a bottle of brandy from his bag and swigs from it*)
Arthur Don't drink all that, Frank..

Frank She told you, did she?

Arthur She mentioned it.

Frank It was a mess.

Spud Got that off; are you ready?

Arthur Just wait on ...

Frank Sorry. Want a swig? I've been drinking all day.

Arthur Not for me ...

Spud I will. Warm my cockles.

He takes the bottle and swigs from it. He then keeps hold of the bottle

Arthur So what's happened?

Frank I've made a right pig's ear of it.

Spud Well, tha's a butcher i'n't tha? Should be good at that.

Arthur Spud, back off, will you, sunshine?

Frank I thought I was in there.

Arthur And aren't you?

Frank No.

Arthur Why?

Frank Because I'm pathetic when it comes to women.

Arthur What's happened?

Frank The meal was OK. But after ... I couldn't think of anything to talk about. I mean she's lived all over the place. I didn't realize, I thought she was like Tina. Anyway, she got talking about where she went to college, and holidays, and I'm like sat there like a spare part, and I'm listening, I'm listening good. I'm sipping the wine. And I'm nodding. I'm nodding that much I'm bloody dizzy. And then she gets on to her and her husband, and all that, and how she left him because she never saw him. And I says, "Why did you leave him if you never saw him? Because when you left him, you'd never see him." And I thought it was funny but she didn't laugh. And then she's on about me being on my own. And I'm legless. I've drunk two bottles of plonk to myself, just sat listening. And she looks at me — them sad eyes — and I think: "This is it." Anyway, she gets up and goes into the room, and I've got this sprig thing, holly 'n' mistletoe in the doorway. She stands there and I kiss her. You know, I just, well, I couldn't help it. She looked so beautiful, Arthur. She looked so lost to me. And so I kissed her again. She didn't move.

Spud And then what?

Frank She left.

Spud Smart.

Frank I feel awful for taking advantage.

Spud You've only kissed her, Frank.

Frank I've invaded her, though.

Arthur You're probably as well out of it.

Frank And how would you know?

Arthur You've been blown out, Frank. It happens to us all. We're all sad cases.

Frank Are you saying I'm a sad case?

Arthur In this instance, yes ——

Frank Because I'm not having that ——

Arthur Hey, Frank, steady.

Frank I'm not having that ——

Arthur Hey, steady.

Frank Not from you.

Arthur Careful, Frank, you've had a drink — careful.

Frank I'll teach you a bloody lesson, mate.

Frank and Arthur begin to square up to each other

I'm not being told I'm a sad case by a trumped-up painter and decorator.

Arthur Aren't you?

Frank No.

Arthur You are.

Frank I'm not having it.

Arthur You'll have it in a minute ...

Frank Come on, then hit me, knock some sense into me. I bloody well need it..

Spud steps in to split them

Spud Wow, wow, steady, steady. It's Christmas, i'n't it? Why don't you kiss and make up?

Frank (*maudlin, drunk*) Kick me when I'm down, Arthur Hoyle, that's what to do, kick me when I'm down. Christmas Day, and I didn't even open my presents.

Silence

Arthur Go home, Frank.

Frank Yeah.

Arthur Just go and see the kids.

Frank I want to. I want to see my kids, Arthur. But she won't let me.

Frank slowly exits

Spud is left with the bottle of brandy

Spud He's the hard man on the side, is he?

Arthur Was.

Spud Oooh, you are going to get hammered.

Arthur Yeah, well ...

Spud One hundred and fifty — nil. I bet you.

Arthur My betting days are over.

Spud I bet you don't even score.

Arthur Give it a rest, will you?

Spud I bet you don't even touch the ball.

Arthur Well, thanks for the encouragement, Spud.

Spud You're useless, if you ask me.

Arthur Well, that about sums it up, I think.

Spud Call it off.

Arthur Too late now.

Spud It's gunna be cold and all tomorrow. Just think of that. The ball'll be like a lump of ice. When you hit the ground, ooohhh, it'll be like playing on broken glass. Ice on the pitch. Your legs'll be a river of blood. Skin, snot all over, teeth everywhere ...

Arthur Listen, Spud. I'll only ask you this once.

Spud What?

Arthur I don't suppose you fancy a game, do you?

Spud Who?

Arthur You?

Spud No.

Arthur I'll play you if you want.

Spud Are you serious?

Arthur Yeah.

Spud It's a bit cold.

Arthur You said you wanted a game, didn't you?

Spud Yeah, but ...

Arthur Could be your big chance.

Spud No.

Arthur Think about it.

Spud No.

Arthur I thought you were dying for a game?

Spud Yeah, but I haven't trained, have I? I mean, I've turned up and nobody's wanted to train me.

Arthur We have had our hands full.

Spud I think I'll stay where I'm safe.

Arthur Where's that?

Spud On the touchline.

Arthur Great. Well thanks, Spud, you and your twenty stone have been a great help.

Spud Besides you're gunna need my experience on the side, aren't you?

Arthur Am I?

Spud Well if it's going to be a blood bath, you'll need a decent bucket and sponge man.

There is a silence; then music

The Lights fade to Black-out

SCENE 4

The clubhouse changing rooms. Boxing Day

Steve, dressed as a fancy dress nurse, is laid out on a bench, asleep under a large coat. Hazel enters, dressed in a winter track suit with her rugby kit on underneath and carrying a sports bag. She sees Steve's body and begins to get undressed. She coughs

Steve (*stirring*) Oh ...

Hazel Steve?

Steve (*revealing his costume*) Oh ...

Hazel You're not playing in that are you?

Steve I don't like playing in anything. I just like rolling about in mud. Time is it? (*He attempts to stand*)

Hazel Nearly eleven.

Steve I feel rough.

Hazel You look lovely.

Steve Thanks.

Hazel On nights, were you?

Steve Ha ha.

Hazel Casualty, was it?

Steve Feels like it. I've only had an hour's sleep.

Hazel You have got some kit, haven't you?

Steve Somewhere.

Hazel You could borrow some of mine.

Steve I'll play like this, I'm not bothered.

Hazel Better get ready.

Steve Don't shout.

Hazel I'm not.

Steve Well somebody is. I'll tell you sommat, you're lucky I actually got here. What a night.

Hazel (*taking off her track suit and getting prepared*) Did you drive?
Steve Dunno.
Hazel So how did you get here?
Steve No idea. I'm going back to sleep. Give us a shout when it's over.
Hazel Steve ...
Steve Good-night.
Hazel Stevie ...
Steve Don't shout, Doctor, some patients are asleep in here. Oh. The room's still spinning. I feel like death warmed up.
Hazel You're not that bad.
Steve I am.
Hazel Need the kiss of life, do you?
Steve I had the kiss of life last night.
Hazel Lucky you.
Steve I'm in love, Hazel.
Hazel Oh yeah, what's he like?
Steve Funny.
Hazel Serious, is it?
Steve For the first time. For the first time in my life I think it's serious.
Hazel You always say that.
Steve Yeah, but ... This is the real thing. She was over from Leeds. Staying at her sister's. This is it. Oh, yes. I have fallen, hook, line and sinker. As soon as I saw her, I knew.
Hazel What did she go as? A doctor?
Steve A rabbit.

Hazel has now completely changed. She bends and moves her leg as if she is suffering from leg pains

Hazel Oh yeah? Hey, give us a hand, Steve, would you? I've got cramp coming on here. Just push my foot back. My calves are stiffening already.

Steve moves to Hazel and holds her leg, manoeuvring it back and forth

Just push ...
Steve That it?
Hazel Harder ...
Steve I can't, it makes my head pound.
Hazel Harder, Steve.
Steve Keep your voice down Hazel ...
Hazel Yeah, yeah, yeah, yeah better, oooohhh ...
Steve Shall I massage it for you ... ?

Arthur and Frank arrive, both in track suits and carrying sports bags. They take in the scene in an instant

Arthur Oh, right.
Hazel Oh, that's better.
Frank (*to Steve*) What's tha supposed to be?
Steve A fairy.
Frank You're right there.
Steve Are you blind, Frank?
Frank So it would seem, yes ...
Hazel How do you feel, Arthur?
Arthur I've felt better.
Hazel Did you sleep?
Arthur On and off.
Steve That's more than I did. I've only had an hour.
Frank It's nothing to brag about.
Steve I'm here though, aren't I?
Arthur Just.
Frank After the game, Hazel, can we ... ?
Hazel Just leave it, eh?
Arthur Steve, get changed.
Steve I am, I am, don't shout.
Hazel He was doing.
Arthur Ay, it looked like it ...

Arthur, Frank and Steve begin to get changed

Steve No Phil?
Arthur Forget him.
Steve Oh good, that leaves four of us. Why don't you lot get off home and I'll play them by myself?
Arthur Just get changed.
Steve This is the last time. And I mean it this time.
Frank Shut up, Steve.
Steve My head's thumping, I feel sick, my stomach's in my mouth ...
Frank Don't talk, then.
Steve My legs are like jelly.
Frank Give it a miss.
Steve My bra's killing me.
Frank Can I borrow some rubbing oil, Hazel?
Hazel Yeah.
Frank I wouldn't ask but I've left mine ...

Hazel It's there. (*She gestures to her bag*)
Frank Right. (*He finds a bottle of oil in Hazel's bag and sets to work*)
Hazel Yeah.
Frank Thanks.
Hazel Quiet, Arthur?
Arthur I'm thinking.
Steve About calling it off ... ?

*Spud enters, dressed in St John's Ambulance uniform and carrying a
bucket and first aid kit. He is full of enthusiasm for the game, in contrast
to the others*

Spud Great day for it. Sun might even break through. Everybody all right?
Colin West's refereeing.
Arthur Great — he's the worst ref in Yorkshire.
Spud He'll want to inspect your boots before you get out there. He's a
stickler, apparently. Oh, an' I've got all the medical stuff, so you needn't
worry about that. And there's an ambulance on standby just in case.
Steve Great.
Spud It's bad underfoot, like concrete. Somebody's bound to break sommat.
Frank Cheers, Spud.
Spud I went to a game once, and one of the lads broke his leg running down
to the pitch. Smart laugh.
Frank Why don't you go and tell the *Cobblers* all this?
Spud I have.
Arthur Got your bucket then, have you?
Spud Yeah, and my sponge.
Hazel Well, whatever happens, Spud, don't put any cold water down my
back, will you?
Spud I'll put it down your front then. Hey, there's a decent crowd and all.
Steve They like a flogging round here. You got any Hedex?
Spud I've got everything in here. Sea sickness tablets, plasters, Diocalm —
stress relief.
Steve Give us one of each.
Spud (*handing tablets to Steve*) There's a raffle. I've got five quid's worth.
And they're selling soup and all.
Steve Get me some, will you? I'll put it down my shorts.
Spud The oxtail's great. I've had ten cups already.
Arthur Have you seen Jim Stone?
Spud Ay, he's as big as a horse. Reg brought him.
Steve What, in a horse box?
Spud In his Merc, funny man.

Phil arrives, carrying a bag. He looks absolutely elated but very tired

Phil (*shouting*) Oh hey, oh hey, oh hey, oh hey, oh hey ...
Steve Philip Hopley, you strange man.
Phil Look who's talking. Just call me Daddy.
All Oooohhhhh.
Phil I can't believe it.
Hazel Oh, congratulations, Phil. (*She kisses him*)
All Oooohhhhh.
Arthur Well done Phil.

The men shake Phil's hand

Frank Nice one.
Phil Six pounds. She is beautiful, Hazel.
Hazel Should you be here?
Phil Her mother said to come. She's got Carole's eyes.
Frank She's got her mother's eyes and her father's car.
Phil Frank, you should've been there.
Frank Oh, thanks.
Phil I think she's got my smile.
Steve (*still wearing his wig and make-up*) Congratulations. Gi's a kiss.
Phil Carole was just ... I mean, you know ...
Hazel What have you called her, Phil?
Steve Phyllis, what else?
Phil Zoë. It means life in Greek.
Hazel I like Zoë as a name.
Phil Zoë Hopley, eh? Sounds good, eh?
Steve Zoë. What is she, a Martian?
Arthur Listen, Phil mate, I'm really pleased for you. Congratulations. Well
    done. I know how long it takes, believe me. We'll all have a drink after.
Phil Let's have a drink now.
Steve Yes, nice one.
Phil I've got some bubbly in my bag. Arthur, wet the baby's head, at least?
    Come on, eh? Let's go out with a bang? Look at this, six bottles of
    champers. (*He produces six bottles of champagne from his bag*) Spud, get
    some plastic cups.
Steve I've got some sounds in my car. Sod the game — let's have a party.
Phil Oh yes, I think so.
Steve Brilliant. I'll put my stockings back on.
Phil Hazel, you'll have a drink, won't you?
Hazel After, maybe.
Phil No, now ...
Spud Hey, shall I get some pizzas sent up?
Frank Where from, on Boxing Day?
Steve There's that place in town.

Spud Leave it with me. I'll get it sorted. (*He produces a mobile phone —
Phil's phone — and makes a call*)

Phil Come on, Arthur, a baby's been born.

Arthur Phil, what can I say...

Phil Life goes on ...

Spud (*into the phone*) I want a number for Mister Pizza, please. ... Cheers.
(*To Arthur, referring to the phone*) These are brilliant, Arthur; you should
get one.

Arthur Listen, hang on, Phil, Spud ...

Phil (*noticing the phone*) Where'd you get that?

Spud What?

Phil That.

Spud It's yours.

Phil I bloody well know that. I've been looking all over for it.

Spud I was looking after it, that's all.

Steve Oh, ay.

Phil You thieving little sod.

Spud Here, have it back.

Phil You can keep it.

Spud Are you joking?

Phil Keep it. Give it me back when you're finished with it. It's a belated
Christmas present.

Spud Cheers, Phil.

Arthur Hang on. Listen, whoa, listen. Look at you. You're like kids.

Spud You're a good bloke, Phil. I'd got you well wrong there.

Phil Let's get some bottles opened. (*He goes back to the champagne*)

Arthur Whoa ... OK. Listen.

Phil Hey, Arthur, I bet Spud took your paint. Didn't you?

Spud I did and all. Did my aunt's shed with it.

Steve Nice one, Spud.

Arthur (*hushing the others*) Whoa, please.

There is a silence

Listen. This is not easy to say. I've been giving it some thought and ... it's
not easy, I never thought I'd ever be saying this.

Frank Saying what? You've said nowt yet.

Arthur I'm going to go to Reg.

Frank What for?

Arthur I'm going to ask him to call the game off.

Hazel What?

Steve Thank God for that. Oh yes, oh yes ...

Arthur I can't do it to you, I can't put you through it. I mean, look at Phil:

he's so happy and I'm making him go out and play against that lot.

Spud Oh, that's ridiculous.

Steve (*to Spud*) You're not even playing.

Spud No, but I've put all this stuff on.

Arthur We're not going to make it. We really are not going to make it. Are we? Not this time. I've got two grand in the Halifax — I'm going to offer him that.

Steve Are you serious?

Arthur Steve, it's finished. If we go out there like this, somebody is going to get hurt. And I mean hurt bad.

Phil Arthur, I'm good for a grand.

Arthur I can't do that, Phil.

Phil It's my only offer.

Arthur Are you sure?

Phil One thousand pounds not to play this game. Maybe two thousand, I'm into anything today.

Arthur I'll take it.

Steve I've got four hundred quid. I'd give you more if I had it.

Phil That's three and a half grand. That's a fair deal. He can't grumble at that, can he?

Frank I'm good for eight hundred quid.

Steve Spud?

Spud I'm not even on t' team.

Frank Bucket man counts.

Spud Thirty quid.

Steve It's better than nothing.

Phil That's four grand: we're laughing.

Steve Hazel, are you in?

Hazel I don't believe I'm hearing this. This is just stupid. We've come this far and you're going to throw it all in?

Frank It's the best way, i'n't it?

Arthur We're not up to it. Look at us.

Hazel So what? So what?

Arthur So what?

Hazel Yeah, so what? What have you turned into? What are you scared of?

Arthur Well, we're not scared of them, I'll tell you that much.

Hazel Aren't you? Looks like you are to me. (*She shouts*) Come on, you pathetic bloody men.

There is a silence

(*Softly*) Come on, Frankie.

Frank (*singing*) Swing low, sweet chariot.

They all join in. Their singing rises to a crescendo

Music

The Lights fade to Black-out, then a blue wash comes up on the set

During the following voice-over, Phil exits

Frank, Hazel, Steve and Arthur strike the clubhouse set and Spud clears the props. The tape extract should be long enough to cover the set strike without ever leaving the stage bare

Ray (*voice over*) So, good-day and welcome to what promises to be a great celebration of Rugby League. I'm sure it's going to be a smashing day, in every sense of the word. Just before the teams come out, can I make a few announcements? Could the owner of car registration number twenty-four-T UPT please shift it, as it is blocking the entrance to the St John's Ambulance tent. Thank you. And will Mr Wallace, Mr Ron Wallace from Upton, go home. Please go home, Ron, your wife has phoned in and she is waiting for you to take her to her sister's ... (*He whispers, obviously not expecting the following to be heard*) Hey, hey, they got any soup left? I'm bloody frozen in here. Bring me a soup, will you? (*In his announcer's voice*) So the raffle will be drawn at half-time, and we will be able to see the stunning Reg Welsh Trophy. (*He whispers*) What?

Man (*voice over*) What do you want?

Ray (*voice over*) What?

Man (*voice over*) Soup.

Ray (*voice over*) What have they got?

Man (*voice over*) All sorts.

Ray (*voice over*) Tomato?

Man (*voice over*) Chicken, I think.

Ray (*voice over*) No tomato?

Man (*voice over*) Tomato's off.

Ray (*voice over*) I'll have oxtail.

Man (*voice over*) There is no oxtail.

Ray (*voice over*) I'll have chicken then. (*In his announcer's voice*) And here they come. The *Wheatsheaf* are out first and they look absolutely devastating.

Man (*voice over*) Do you want any bread?

Ray (*voice over*) Two slices.

Music plays

The Lights fade to Black-out

SCENE 5

The pitch

The Lights come slowly up on the Wheatsheaf *team — Frank, Phil, Arthur, Hazel and Steve — all dressed in their kit and ready for the game. Spud stands on the touchline at the back of the stage. There are several rugby balls on stage*

Steve Look at 'em. They've got bigger.
Arthur Don't think about it.
Phil There's a decent turn-out.
Arthur Can anybody see Doreen?
Hazel You don't expect her to come, do you?
Arthur You never know.
Frank I want you to know, Hazel, that I'm only doing this for you.
Arthur We all are.
Hazel Look at the size of 'em. They've got veins on their veins.
Frank Looks like they've been doing some serious training.
Steve So have we. Not. They look like the bloody Gladiators.
Phil Maybe we should have invited them in for a drink?
Hazel I think that champagne's gone to my head.
Steve It's gone to my legs.
Frank We might be the only team ever to play whilst under the influence.
Phil I doubt it.
Arthur We shouldn't have drunk all six bottles.
Spud (*shouting*) Up on 'em, *Wheatsheaf*, nice and flat. Man and ball.
Steve I hope he's not going to shout like that during the game — it's embarrassing.
Arthur Right, lads, come on. Let's get right up at 'em from the kick-off.

Arthur and Phil position themselves. Hazel, Steve and Frank become Cobblers *and run* DS *with their backs to the audience. They growl*

"Frank" Get it kicked.
"Steve" Come on, Skinny.
"Frank" We're gunna eat you ...
"Steve" Come, Arthur ...
Arthur Ready, Phil?
Phil Get it kicked, man, I'm bloody freezing ...

A whistle is blown

Arthur Up on 'em, quick.

Arthur kicks the ball DL *and it is caught by Hazel*

"Hazel" Good as a pass.
"Frank" Go on, Nutter ...
"Steve" Straight through.
Phil Nutter. What a stupid name.
Arthur Your man, Phil.
Phil I've got him ... You're mine, Nutter!

Hazel runs in a straight line with the ball and is tackled by Phil. In the tackle she "nuts" Phil full in the face

Phil Ooooohhh.
Arthur Referee?
"Hazel" Call that a tackle, you wimp? Come on, then.

Hazel plays the ball to Frank; he passes it on to Steve who is standing outside him. Steve acts as a pivot; Frank comes around on the overlap and takes the ball from him

"Frank" My ball, Brent.

Arthur runs for Steve, who throws the ball back to Frank. Arthur attempts to tackle Steve but gets hit in the neck and falls to the floor

Spud Referee ... Come on, man.

Phil runs traversely across and edges off Frank, who turns the ball inside to Hazel; she runs with the ball UC *and scores under the post. As soon as she scores she turns and becomes the "real" Hazel*

Hazel Come on, lads.
Phil I think they're playing dirty.
Hazel You all right, Arthur?
Arthur I would be, if I could see.
Phil Four-nil.
Arthur Are they taking the conversion?
Frank They're not bothering.
Steve That's how confident they are.
Phil Four-nil in less than a minute. They're a lot fitter. They're faster.
Hazel And I bet they're not drunk.
Arthur Come on, up and at 'em.
Steve They're not messing about, are they?

Spud Come on, *Wheatsheaf*. Flat, stay flat. Don't let 'em bust through.
Arthur Watch for the simple stuff.
Frank Don't get drawn.
Steve Stay wide.
Hazel I'm covering two men here.
Steve Lucky you.
Hazel Thanks.
Arthur They're playing simple copy-book stuff. Zone defence. They're only human.
Steve Only just.
Phil Try and force them into the corners near the line. Keep the score down. Right.
All Right.
Spud (*shouting*) Try and force 'em into the corners. Keep the score down.
Steve We know, Spud.
Arthur Four-nil, our kick, come on.

Phil, Frank and Steve become Cobblers. *Arthur and Hazel remain* Wheatsheaf

Arthur Don't get drawn.

The ball goes to Frank, who moves across UL *and heads towards Phil*

"Phil" Scissors, Jim ...

Phil and Frank execute a successful scissors move; Arthur puts a tackle in on Frank, who grabs him and pushes him down into the ground. Hazel now has to cover two men, Phil and Steve, the latter outside the former

    (*Teasing Hazel with the ball*) Come on, darling, not scared are you?
Hazel Just play the game ...

Eventually Hazel tackles Phil but he passes to Steve. Phil attempts to kiss Hazel. Steve runs into the corner and they all become Wheatsheaf *once more*

Phil Well played, Hazel, you forced him into the corner.
Frank Yeah, well played, Hazel.
Arthur Creep.
Frank She did well.
Arthur Well played, Hazel. Good work.
Hazel It's all I could do.
Arthur Let's try and keep the score down this half.
Steve It's eight-nil already. We've only been playing for a minute.

Phil If they continue to score at this rate it'll be eighty-nil by half-time.
Frank Where's all our supporters?
Steve Maybe they couldn't come.
Hazel What, both of 'em?
Steve Very funny.
Frank Let's get 'em going. We might be able to live off their energy.
Steve We'll not be able to live off mine, I'll tell you.
Frank (*to the crowd*) Come on the 'Sheaf!
Spud Come on the 'Sheaf ...
Phil Leave it, Frank, you'll only encourage him.
Arthur Come on, Frank, we're playing Rugby, not community singing.
Spud Come on the 'Sheaf.
Arthur Right, face up ...
Hazel They're just laughing at us: look ...

They all turn around and become Cobblers, *laugh once and turn back*

Phil Vary the kick, Arthur.
Arthur Cross kick. Kick and chase.

Steve, Hazel and Frank become Cobblers. *Arthur kicks* DC. *Frank runs* r *and is tackled by Phil*

Phil Get down.
Arthur Nice one, Phil.
Spud (*in a singsong voice*) Come on the 'Sheaf.

Hazel comes from DL, *takes the ball from Frank, and runs into Arthur. Hazel plays the ball to Steve, who runs* L *into Phil who has covered ground around the back. Phil is injured. Frank gets the ball and starts to circumvent the* DS *area. Arthur attempts a tackle, but is handed off in the face. Hazel is out wide. It remains for Steve to tackle Frank*

Arthur Your man, Steve.
Steve Oh, no.
Phil Come on, Steve, get that shoulder in.
Arthur Remember the tyre.
Steve What?

Steve dips his shoulder and successfully tackles Frank. Steve lays on top of Frank

Steve I did it. I did it.

Hazel Tackle, Steve.

Steve Can I go now, Arthur?

Arthur No. It's our ball.

Steve What? Impossible. You mean we're going to touch it?

Phil Fourth tackle, turn around. Our ball.

Hazel Come on, Steve, get it played.

Spud (*in a singsong voice*) Come on the '*Sheeeaaaaafffff*.

Frank becomes Jim Stone DR. *He faces Steve, Phil and Arthur, with Hazel on the wing*

Steve (*playing the ball to Phil*) Here, you have it.

Phil catches the ball, runs forward, sees Frank, turns back and passes to Hazel; she runs forward and sees Frank, who growls. She runs back. Phil, Steve, Hazel and Arthur stand UC

Hazel There's no way through.

Phil It's a blanket defence.

Steve We're trapped, we're trapped.

Hazel Here, you have it. (*She passes to Phil*)

Phil I don't want it.

Hazel They're coming for us.

Arthur There's only one thing we can do.

Steve Give 'em the money. Just give 'em the money.

Arthur Watch this.

Spud (*in a sing-song voice*) Come on the '*Sheeeeeaaaaaaafffffff*. Good
  buddy.

A musical underscore begins to play

In the following sequence, everyone goes into slow motion. Arthur sets off in a slow motion run towards Frank. He looks to be doing very well. He is about to side-step Frank when Frank stiff-arms him and he drops to the floor. Frank becomes the "real" Frank

The action returns to real speed

Blood pours from Arthur's mouth. He has lost some teeth

Frank Penalty.

All Penalty, surely ... Come on Ref ... Nearly took his head off ... (*etc.*)

Hazel You're not wearing black for a funeral, you know, Ref?

Steve Hey, he might be.
Frank Are you all right, Arth?
Phil Frank, his teeth are falling out.
Frank I think they're playing it dirty.
Phil Brilliant, Doctor Watson.
Frank If they want to play dirty, so can I.
Steve Get Spud on ... (*He calls*) Spud ...
Hazel The magic sponge is coming, Arth.
Steve (*holding up three fingers*) How many fingers am I holding up?
Arthur Arghhh ...
Steve Three, Arth, three fingers.
Spud All right, Arth?
Arthur Argghh.
Spud I told you somebody'd get hurt, didn't I?
Phil We've got a man down here, Ref.
Hazel He's ignoring us.
Steve Hey up, Ref, you bald-headed bas ——
Phil Leave it, Steve, don't make matters any worse.
Arthur Arghhh, take the money, stop the game ... game ... Stop the game,
     I wanna get off.
Spud He's delirious.
Steve Sounds like sense to me.
Spud We'll have to get him off.
Frank Will time be added on?
Phil Second half.
Spud Come on, Arth, let's have you in the tent, shall we?
Hazel Will he be all right?
Spud Ar, once he spits his teeth out he'll be laughing.

  Phil, Spud and Frank carry Arthur off. He is totally out of it.

  Steve and Hazel find a moment's repose

Steve We've had it.
Hazel I know.
Steve There's no way we're going to come back now.
Hazel Come on, Stevie boy, chin up.
Steve Typical i'n't it?
Hazel What?
Steve I actually fall in love, then somebody rearranges my features.
Hazel They haven't yet.
Steve They will do, though. I got an awful feeling about it. I'm going to go
     home with my nostrils where my ears used to be.
Hazel What's she called then?

Steve Who?

Hazel This new woman?

Steve Oh, er ...

Hazel You must know her name?

Steve I do.

Hazel Well, what is it?

Steve Lois, I think — no, hang on, I think it's Angie ...

Hazel You think?

Steve Yeah, yeah ...

Hazel You're making this up, aren't you?

Steve What?

Hazel You know what I think? I think you haven't got a woman. I think it's all talk.

Steve Oh yeah. As if?

Phil and Frank return

Phil Right, we'll have to re-plan.

Steve Yeah, let's open a transport caff.

Hazel Be sensible.

Steve I was being, believe me.

Frank Arthur's gunna be out for the rest of the game.

Steve Oh brilliant. Brilliant. (*To the* Cobblers) Hey, Jim, me next, please, will you? Take me out, put me in hospital.

Phil Right, Steve, play hooker.

Steve Hooker?

Phil Hazel, prop.

Hazel Right.

Phil I'll have to play scrum half, stand off and centre.

Frank And winger?

Phil No. We'll cut the wingers out.

Steve That'll fool 'em.

Frank We're going to have to work twice as hard. Cover the zones. Make every tackle count.

Phil Remember it's a man and a third each.

Frank Somebody's gunna pay for this.

Hazel Come on then, Frank, let's see you get in there and show them what you're made of.

Steve Whatever happens don't pass to me. I'm dead. I'm a corpse; just ignore me.

Phil Come on, Steve, you're as good as the rest of us.

Steve Is there any champagne left?

Phil Come on. Short kick, this time. Right?

All Right.

Phil and Frank remain as the Wheatsheaf. *Steve and Hazel become* Cobblers. *The kick goes to Hazel who is tackled by Frank. Frank grabs Hazel in preparation for a head butt*

Phil Nut him, Frank.

Frank nuts Hazel in slow motion, but comes off worse; he holds his head and falls to the floor. Hazel passes the ball to Steve — an obvious forward pass — and Steve scores. They all become the Wheatsheaf. *Hazel gets the ball*

Frank Forrad, man.
Steve Come on, Ref, it was a mile forward.
Hazel (UC *with the ball*) Ref, why didn't you blow for it?

A long hard whistle indicates half-time

Phil Half-time.
Steve Twelve-nil. Better than I expected.
Hazel We're doing OK, considering.
Frank You're playing well, Hazel.
Hazel Thanks, Frank.
Frank Yeah. You're playing well and all, Steve.
Steve I'm all over the shop, I'm seeing double.
Ray (*voice over*) Well the ... er ... er ... winner of the raffle is Mr Wallace. Mr Ron Wallace from Upton. But ... er ... er ... we understand he's gone to his wife's sister's. So we will be presenting the second prize of twenty-five pounds to Mr Layton after the match. Thank you.
Steve I wish I could go home.
Phil Well, it's only ten more minutes so we might as well just go on and stroll about.
Hazel That's all Steve's been doing anyway.
Steve No wonder, is there? I was half sloshed when I turned up. My head's thumping.
Frank Twelve-nil. Not bad.
Steve It's only money, isn't it?
Hazel It's never over till it's over.
Phil It is when it's over.
Steve I'm sure they're playing with fourteen.
Frank You're learning sommat here, Stevie boy. Nothing is fair in this life.

Arthur enters, bandaged up and groggy

Arthur What's the score?
Hazel Are you OK?
Frank Twelve-nil.
Arthur Who to?
Frank Who to?
Phil Arthur, you can't play, mate, you're all over the place.
Arthur Twelve-nil? We've still got a chance.
Steve We've never had a chance, never.
Arthur We were getting drawn far too early.
Hazel Arth, we're going to lose, we've as good as lost already.
Arthur That's what they want you to think. They want to keep us down, break our spirits.
Frank I think they want to break our necks, really.
Arthur Come on, up and at 'em.
Phil No, Arth.
Arthur No?
Phil No. That's it for me. These lot aren't interested in playing rugby. They want to injure someone. It was the same at Loughborough. Half the teams wanted to play and half just wanted a scrap. There's no point playing against these, they just want to mix it up.
Arthur Well, let's mix it back.
Phil What with? We've got a woman, you're barely conscious and all of us are half cut.
Hazel Come on, are we playing or not?
Phil Don't you start.
Frank Well, let's just play and have a laugh.
Arthur Oh that'd look good, we would be the laughing stock then.
Steve Let's just play and not tackle 'em.
Phil What's new?

There is a silence

Hazel You can't play any more, Arthur. It's too dangerous.

There is a pause

Arthur I'm OK, honest, I'm fine.

   Spud enters wearing rugby kit

Spud Bloody hell, the things I do. Come on then, Phil, spin one out to me.

Phil spins the ball to Spud who catches it with real skill

I can't bear to watch. I've got to get involved. Right, Arth, where do you
want me?

Arthur Are you serious?

Spud Course I am.

Arthur Right then. Let's re-organize. Spud, you play prop.

Frank He could play the whole front row.

Spud No, I'm not playing prop, it hurts your neck.

Arthur But you're a natural.

Spud No, I'm a natural scrum half.

Arthur What?

Steve Let him play anywhere, Arth.

Arthur Spud, play anywhere.

Spud Roger Spodge.

A whistle blows for the second half

Arthur Come on, we're still in with a chance.

Phil They've brought two subs on.

Hazel Are they Aussies?

Arthur There isn't an amateur on their side.

Frank They don't like the look of Spud.

Steve Come on, Meatloaf, frighten 'em to death.

Spud Which way are we playing?

Hazel That way.

Spud Oh, cheers, Hazel. My eyes aren't what they were.

Steve Why, what were they?

Phil Steve, shut up and face up.

Arthur Their kick to us.

*They line up diagonally across the stage in this order from L to R: Arthur,
Steve, Frank, Spud, Phil, Hazel. Arthur holds the ball as though he has caught
it from a* Cobblers *kick*

Frank Watch the short one.

Steve Taken, Arth.

Arthur (*passing the ball to Steve*) Steve.

Steve (*passing the ball to Frank*) Frank.

Frank (*preparing to pass the ball to Spud*) Spud.

Spud Ar, not to me, don't pass to me. (*He laughs*) Only joking, pass then ...

Frank passes the ball to Phil, who runs DS *and performs a scissor move with
Hazel. Spud unwittingly drifts forward and Hazel passes the ball to him*

Spud Ar ... No ... (*He freezes to the spot*)
Steve Run, Spud.
Phil Run.

Spud looks around hesitantly

Hazel Run, Spud.

Spud runs around the stage

Steve Other way, Spud.

Spud weaves uncontrollably. Arthur and Frank become Cobblers *and eventually put a tackle in on Spud, who ends up on the floor trying to get back up*

"Arthur" Play the ball, fatman.
Spud Eh?
"Arthur" Play the ball.
Spud Let me get up, then. (*He gets up*)
Phil Play the ball, Spud.
Spud Fourth tackle, innit? Their ball. (*He hands the ball to the* Cobblers)
Phil No, it's the first tackle.

Arthur takes the ball and scores, US. He then becomes the "real" Arthur

Steve Force him into the corner.
Arthur (*turning furiously to Spud*) What are you doing?
Spud Fourth tackle, wasn't it?
Arthur No.
Phil Can't you count?
Spud Sorry, I thought ...
Hazel Sixteen-nil.
Steve That's it now, surely.
Hazel Sixteen-nil.
Arthur (*to Spud*) Are you bloody stupid?
Spud No.
Arthur You could have fooled me.
Spud I've come on to help you and you're playing hell.
Arthur Oh, forget it.
Spud Just don't say I'm stupid.
Arthur Forget it.
Spud (*grabbing Arthur*) Just don't say I'm stupid. It was a mistake. OK?

Arthur OK, OK.

Steve, Phil and Frank become Cobblers. *Arthur, Spud and Hazel face up*

Hazel Come Arthur, our kick.
"Frank" Come on, stupid.
"Phil" Give it to that big 'un.
"Steve" Give it to that stupid 'un.

The whistle blows

Arthur kicks the ball to Phil who runs forward and is tackled by Hazel. Phil plays the ball to Steve who passes it out to Frank (Jim Stone)

"Phil" Go on, Jim, straight through that big 'un.
Spud Get down.

Jim/Frank runs around the DS *area, and makes a bee-line for Spud. He charges into Spud but Spud body-checks him and sends him sailing into the air, held by the others. Jim/Frank drops the ball*

Hazel Nice one, Spud.
Spud Not bad, eh? Hey, Ref, call this one an ambulance.
Steve Ten-ten, Spud. Jim, you're an ambulance.
Hazel Get the ball.
Spud Eh?
Hazel Get the ball.
Spud Oh right ... smart. (*He picks up the ball and begins to move forward*)

Arthur tries to tackle Spud but ends up over his shoulder. Frank holds Spud around the waist

Phil (*nearby*) Spud, pass ... Spud ...
Spud What?
Phil Pass.
Spud Have you seen this, two men on me?
Phil Yeah, great, just pass ...
Spud Who to?
Phil To me, to me, to me.
Spud You wouldn't pass to me.
Phil Just pass it ...

Spud releases a pass to Phil, who side-steps Steve with a man to beat

Phil A man to beat off one foot. (*He scores*) A try, a try underneath the posts. I do not believe it. I just do not believe it. Look at me, I'm crying. I'm crying.
Hazel (*kissing Phil*) Brilliant, Phil.
Steve (*kissing Phil*) Well done, Phil mate.
Arthur Nice one, Phil.
Phil No kiss from you, Arth?
Arthur Come here. (*He kisses Phil, then looks at the* Cobblers) So what, I love him. I love 'em all.
Frank Steady on, Arth. Brilliant side-step?
Hazel What side-step? He just stumbled.
Frank Good on you, Phil.
Phil Cheers, Frank.

Spud takes the kick

Hazel Spud's kicked it; sixteen-six. Come on, face up. Their kick.
Phil Watch the grubber.

The ball is thrown on to Hazel US. *She catches the ball but is tackled by Steve. She plays the ball to Phil, who runs* DS *with Frank on his* L *and Arthur on his* R. *The ball is played to Arthur; then we go into slow motion. Arthur runs through what seems like a maze of players, makes a number of great hand-offs, and scores in the* UL *corner*

Arthur Yes, thank you, that'll do. (*He makes a gesture to the crowd*) That's for you, Doreen. Wherever you are.
Frank Brilliant try, Arth.
Spud Superb try.
Hazel (*kissing Arthur*) Arthur, you're a star.
Frank Sixteen-ten.
Steve Three minutes left.
Phil Watch the long kick. Spud, drop back.

The whistle blows

All the Wheatsheaf *move back* US *except Spud, who lingers* C. *The ball is thrown on and comes to Spud*

Spud My ball. A drop kick.
Phil From our own twenty-two — don't be stupid. Sorry, sorry — I didn't mean it ...
Steve You'll never do it.
Hazel Let's run it.
Spud No. I've got this. Watch this. (*He launches the drop kick*)

In reality, the ball disappears behind Spud's back but the actors "watch" it fly. It takes an age before it gets to the other end of the pitch. They all respond as the ball goes over. Then there is a silence

Steve I do not believe it.
Spud Smart — see that?
Hazel Sixteen-eleven.
Arthur Hey, look, Reg isn't laughing now ...
Frank Two minutes left; they'll try and keep us out ...

Frank, Spud and Steve become Cobblers. *Arthur has the ball, with Phil outside him and Hazel outside Phil*

Phil Watch the kick, Arth, it's a nasty one.
"Cobblers" On 'em ... flat.
Arthur My ball.
Hazel Keep it alive, Arthur.
"Frank" Smack 'em.
"Spud" Keep 'em out.

Arthur runs forward and is tackled by Frank. Frank passes to Phil who is tackled by Steve, Steve passes to Hazel who is tackled by Spud; Arthur takes the ball from Hazel and dives for the line, but he is dragged back by the Cobblers. *Arthur gets up to play the ball, with Spud marking him. There is no way past Spud so Arthur plays the ball to Hazel, who crawls through Spud's legs. As she does this, Spud grabs her and knees her in the head; despite this, Hazel stumbles forward and scores. She hits the floor, unconscious*

All Yeeesss.
"Spud" That wasn't a try.
Arthur It was, you look in the Green 'Un.
Steve Great try, Hazel.
Phil We've got 'em. We can beat 'em.
Frank Sixteen-fifteen.
Phil One minute to play.
Steve I don't believe it.
Arthur Well played Hazel. Hazel?
Spud (*attending to Hazel*) Arth, we'd better get her off. She's out cold.
Frank (*calling to the Cobblers*) You dirty sods.
Arthur Hazel, Hazel? Is she OK?
Frank Somebody's gunna pay for this.
Spud Let's get her off, man. She's concussed.
Steve Will she be OK?

Spud She's just taken a bang.
Frank Spud, she will be all right, won't she?
Spud How the bloody hell do I know?

Spud exits

Steve I knew it. I knew somebody'd get hurt.
Frank Do you think she'll be OK?
Phil Just calm down Frank, OK?
Frank It was a bloody stupid idea letting her play in the first place.
Arthur Don't look at me.
Frank It was your idea.
Arthur I know, I know.
Steve I knew somebody'd get hurt.
Arthur Shut up, Steve.
Steve I'm just glad it's not me.
Arthur (*strokes Hazel's head*) It's OK, kid. It's OK. (*To Frank*) I think she's
   just taken a knock.
Steve She was playing well and all.

*Spud returns with a stretcher and blanket. He puts Hazel on to the
stretcher; his competence as a St John's Ambulance man is evident*

Hazel is carried off by Steve and Spud

Arthur Frank?
Phil Forget it, you two.
Frank Don't say it.
Arthur Sorry.
Frank I just hope she's all right, for your sake.
Phil She'll be OK, Frank.
Arthur Sorry, Frank.
Frank Just get it kicked.
Phil The last kick of the game.
Frank Again.
Arthur I'll take it.
Phil No way.
Arthur It's a straightforward kick.
Frank That's what you said last time.
Arthur I'm taking it.
Phil Please.
Frank Let Phil take it.

Steve enters

Steve Let me take it?
All No.
Frank How is she?
Steve It doesn't look good. You should see Spud, he's brilliant.
Arthur (*hands the ball to Phil*) Don't bloody miss.

Phil places the ball, taking his time

Steve Come on, Phil.
Phil Ssshh, let me concentrate.
Frank Come on, Phil.
Arthur Don't miss, Phil. Please.
Steve Don't hook it.

Spud enters US

Phil is about to kick when ...

Spud Don't slice it.

Phil takes time to prepare. It is agonizing for the others to wait for such a time

Frank Come on, Phil, it'll be dark soon.
All Ssssh.

They watch. Phil takes the kick. He misses. They are all utterly wasted. Phil is frozen. Arthur looks as if he wants to kill Phil

Phil Oooohhhhh.
Frank Oh no.
Steve I'm gunna be sick.
Spud Oh ... (*He cries*) You stupid sod ...
Phil Hit the post.
Arthur (*slowly*) I'll kill yer ...
Frank The last kick of the bloody game.
Steve Still sixteen-fifteen.
Arthur I'll kill yer.
Phil Hit the post ... Arhhhhh ... (*He falls to his knees*)
Frank That's it.
Steve How long left, Ref?
Arthur How long ...

Spud (*screaming*) How long left, you little ...
Frank Leave it, Spud.
Steve A minute's injury time.
Phil A minute left, a minute left.
Arthur That's it ... (*He wails*) Ooohh.
Frank (*to the* Cobblers) Get it kicked ... come on, man, kick it.
Arthur Watch the kick, cover across.
Phil Sorry, Arth.
Arthur (*growling*) Grrrrrrrrrr!
Steve They'll kick long.
Frank They're playing for time. Come on, get it kicked.
Arthur Drop back.
Steve Spud, drop back.
Phil Watch the short one.

Spud collects the ball

Frank Drop kick, Spud, drop kick for a draw.
Spud No chance ... (*To the* Cobblers) Right, come on then ...

Spud dummies a drop kick, then runs forward, setting off on a mind-blowingly difficult central charge. The scene goes into slow motion. During the following sequence, Arthur, Phil, Steve and Frank speak Wheatsheaf *lines but move as Spud's* Cobbler *opposition*

Phil Go, Spud.
Steve Pass, Spud.

Spud hands off the tackle

Frank Go, Spud ...
Arthur Fifteen seconds left ...
Phil Pass ... pass ...
Steve Let it go, Spud ...
Spud No way ...
Frank Nine seconds ...

A punch lands on Spud

Spud Watch the punching, Ref ...
Arthur Seven seconds ...
Phil Pass you stupid sod, pass, pass, pass ...
Arthur Five seconds ...

Frank Keep going ...

Arthur Four seconds ...

Steve Head down, Spud ...

Phil I played for Loughborough first team. Pass to me — I'm a dad! I'm in here.

Arthur Oh no, I can see my life passing before me ...

Steve Use your power ...

Frank Three seconds ... three seconds to go.

Spud Never say never, that's what I say; there's allus hope, there's allus some spirit burning deep down inside.

Phil Shut up and pass ...

Arthur Two seconds ...

Phil Pass ...

Spud passes to Phil who, in a horrible mix-up, appears to fumble the pass. All the Wheatsheaf *scream*

Black-out

Music plays

Scene 6

The clubhouse. Later

The Wheatsheaf *team, except Hazel, is on stage. They are all utterly exhausted. Phil sits catching his breath. Steve lies on a bench with a wrapped video beside him. Frank is crying. Spud is large and silent. Arthur sobs softly. All groan and grunt with aches and pains*

There is a silence

Frank I wonder how Hazel's doing?

Further silence

Phil I am absolutely shattered. I've shattered myself.

Spud What sort of a ref was he then?

Arthur Forget it.

Steve I can't talk.

Arthur (*in disbelief*) Yes, you can.

Steve But I can't even pick my arms up. I can't even breathe. I'm that tired.

Frank Do you think she'll be all right, Spud?

Spud Oh ar.

Arthur Well that's it then.
Phil "Funny game, Saint".
Spud That's it then, is it?
Arthur That's it.

Steve gets up to move but is struck with a bad attack of leg cramp

Steve Oh, oh, oh; typical, innit? I get cramp off the pitch.

There is a silence

Frank I don't believe it.

Hazel enters. She is groggy and bruised about the face, with a black eye

Hazel Arth?
Arthur Yeah?
Hazel I think Doreen wants a word.
Arthur Oh.
Hazel Yeah.
Arthur Where is she?
Hazel Over by the cars.
Arthur I'd better go and face the music.
Hazel So what happened?
Spud You caught a knee at the side of your face.
Hazel I mean with the game.
Phil Don't you know?
Hazel I've been flat out, Phil.
Steve Good job Frank didn't know.
Arthur (*inordinately*) Oh, we beat 'em.
Frank I don't believe it.
Hazel What?
Arthur Phil scored in the last minute.
Spud After I had done all the work and unselfishly passed.
Hazel (*sitting*) You're joking?
Phil No.
Hazel What?
Arthur I'd better go and see Doreen.
Hazel I think she wants you back home, Arth.
Arthur Yippee, another Christmas present.
Steve Oh ar ... Arthur. Nearly forgot. Here you are. (*He offers Arthur the video wrapped in paper*) We've sort of clubbed together to get you something. Just to sort of say thanks.
Arthur Oh, I wonder what it is?

Steve You'll never guess.

Arthur "A Hundred and One Top Rugby League Tries"?

Steve Who told you?

Arthur That's the problem with this team. No communication.

Steve Eh?

Spud So when are this lot training again, Arthur?

Arthur That's it for me.

Frank Get away.

Arthur No, that's it for me. No more. I'm gunna take up golf, I think

Phil You're joking?

Arthur No.

Steve Tha's jesting i'n't tha?

Arthur No ... that's it for me, lads. I won't be putting you through it any more. You can train when you want ... Anyway.

Pause

I'd better go and see how Doreen is.

Arthur very slowly hobbles off

There is a silence

Phil He'll be back.

Frank If she lets him.

Hazel Well, at least you survived it, Stevie. You'll be able to see that new woman of yours now.

Steve (*caught out*) What? Oh yeah, yeah.

Spud I'd better get off and all.

Phil Are you going to come out in the New Year, Spud?

Spud No.

Phil Oh, right.

Spud Only joking, Phil. I might turn out, tha never knows. I'll get off then, take care. Have a good New Year.

Steve See you then, good bud.

Spud Ar, that's a Roge, Stick Man.

Spud exits

Silence. There is a current of real laughter, almost excitement, under the following dialogue

Hazel Come on, Frank.

Frank What?

Hazel Cheer up.

Frank After five years of playing in snow, hail and rain we have actually won
a game for the first time ... I don't believe it.

Phil It's the shock, Frank.

Frank Bloody hell, I don't believe it.

*Frank breaks into a laugh. Phil joins him. Hazel cannot laugh because her
jaw is killing her. Phil finds this funny. Steve finds Hazel's aching jaw funny,
but then is caught with a very bad case of leg cramp. He begins to call out.
They all laugh*

Music plays

The Lights fade to Black-out

CURTAIN

FURNITURE AND PROPERTY LIST

ACT I
SCENE 1

On stage: Rugby balls
             Arthur's sports bag

Personal: **Arthur**: hat

SCENE 2

Off stage: Tape recorder (**Ray**)

SCENE 3

On stage: Television set

Off stage: Seats (**Phil**)
             Video player (**Steve**)
             Electric fire (**Phil**)
             Crate of low-alcohol beer in cans (**Arthur**)
             Plastic bag. *In it*: videos (**Arthur**)
             Bags of "goodies" (**Frank**)

SCENE 4

On stage: Rugby balls

Off stage: Large umbrella (**Steve**)
             Bag, street cone and rubber tube (**Arthur**)
             Cases, plastic bags and videos (**Doreen**)

ACT II
SCENE 1

On stage: **Phil**'s sports bag. *In it*: mobile phone
             Hazel's sports bag. *In it*: wrapped-up video
             Rugby balls

Off stage: Tape recorder (**Ray**)
                Bucket (**Spud**)

SCENE 2

On stage: Chairs
               Table
               Trophy
               Bottle of champagne
               Two champagne glasses for **Ray** and **Reg**

SCENE 3

On stage: Rugby balls
               Windscreen scraper, can of de-icer spray for **Arthur**

Off stage: Plastic bags containing slippers, luminous rugby ball (**Spud**)
               Bag containing bottle of brandy (**Frank**)

SCENE 4

Off stage: Sports bag (**Arthur**)
               Sports bag (**Frank**)
               Sports bag containing bottle of rubbing oil (**Hazel**)
               Bucket, first aid kit, **Phil**'s mobile phone (**Spud**)
               Bag containing six bottles of champagne (**Phil**)

SCENE 5

On stage: Rugby balls

Off stage: Stretcher and blanket (**Spud**)

Personal: Blood capsule (**Arthur**)

SCENE 6

On stage: Bench
               Wrapped video for **Steve**

LIGHTING PLOT

Various interior and exterior settings
Practical fittings required: TV screen and fireglow effects

ACT I, SCENE 1

To open: Darkness

Cue 1	**Musical overture** *Bring up dim exterior lighting*	(Page 1)
Cue 2	**Music** *Black-out*	(Page 8)

ACT I, SCENE 2

To open: General exterior lighting

Cue 3	**Music** *Black-out*	(Page 11)

ACT I, SCENE 3

To open: General interior lighting

Cue 4	**Phil** plugs in fire *Fireglow effect*	(Page 12)
Cue 5	**Phil**: "... Frank starts weeping all over us." *Fade overhead lighting; bring up TV screen* *and fireglow effects*	(Page 20)

ACT I, SCENE 3A

To open: As end of Act I, Scene 3

Cue 6	**All**: " ... Rocky Rocky Rocky Rocky Rocky." *Black-out*	(Page 20)

ACT I, Scene 3B

To open: General interior lighting with TV screen and fireglow effects

Cue 7	**Phil**: " ... then we can all go home!"	(Page 22)
	Black-out	

ACT I, Scene 3C

To open: Cold general lighting with fireglow effect

Cue 8	**Phil** unplugs electric fire	(Page 25)
	Cut fireglow effect	
Cue 9	Music	(Page 26)
	Black-out	

ACT I, Scene 4

To open: General exterior lighting: rain effect

Cue 10	**Phil**: "You lads go, I'm off home."	(Page 31)
	Lightning flash	
Cue 11	Music	(Page 38)
	Black-out	

ACT II

ACT II, Scene 1

To open: Dim general exterior lighting

Cue 12	**Arthur**: "Frank'll be waiting for you."	(Page 47)
	Black-out	

ACT II, Scene 2

To open: General interior lighting

Cue 13   Music plays   (Page 49)
            Black-out

ACT II, Scene 3

To open: General exterior lighting

Cue 14   Music   (Page 55)
            Black-out

ACT II, Scene 4

To open: General interior lighting

Cue 15   Music plays   (Page 62)
            Black-out, then bring up blue wash

Cue 16   Taped dialogue finishes; music   (Page 62)
            Black-out

ACT II, Scene 5

To open: Slowly bring up general exterior lighting

Cue 17   All the *Wheatsheaf* scream   (Page 80)
            Black-out

ACT II, Scene 6

To open: General interior lighting

Cue 18   They all laugh. Music   (Page 83)
            Black-out

EFFECTS PLOT

ACT I

Cue 1   Before play starts   (Page 1)
Musical overture

Cue 2   Lights come up   (Page 1)
Wind howls (throughout scene)

Cue 3   **Arthur** jogs off   (Page 8)
Music

Cue 4   **Ray**: " ... and may the best team win."   (Page 11)
Music

Cue 5   **Phil**: "If you can get some more players, yeah."   (Page 26)
Music

Cue 6   Lights come up on SCENE 4   (Page 26)
Rain and thunder

Cue 7   **Phil**: "You lads go, I'm off home."   (Page 31)
Roll of thunder; music

Cue 8   **Spud** exits   (Page 33)
Music

Cue 9   **Doreen** exits   (Page 37)
Christmas carols; snow effect

Cue 10   **Arthur** exits   (Page 38)
Music

ACT II

Cue 11   **Spud**: "Hey, come on, be right, he said imagine."   (Page 44)
Mobile phone rings

Cue 12   Black-out   (Page 47)
Music

Cue 13   **Reg**: " ... everything is personal."   (Page 49)
            Music

Cue 14   **Spud:** " ... bucket and sponge man." Silence   (Page 55)
            Music

Cue 15   The singing rises to a crescendo   (Page 62)
            Music

Cue 16   Blue wash comes up on set   (Page 62)
            Dialogue as p. 62; then music

Cue 17   **Phil**: "Get it kicked, man, I'm bloody freezing ..."   (Page 63)
            Whistle blows

Cue 18   **Spud:** "Good buddy."   (Page 67)
            Musical underscore begins

Cue 19   **Hazel**: "Ref, why didn't you blow for it?"   (Page 70)
            Whistle blows long and hard

Cue 20   **Steve**: " ... I'm seeing double."   (Page 70)
            Dialogue as p.70

Cue 21   **Spud**: "Roger Spodge."   (Page 72)
            Whistle blows

Cue 22   **"Steve"**: "Give it to that stupid 'un."   (Page 74)
            Whistle blows

Cue 23   **Phil**: "Spud, drop back."   (Page 75)
            Whistle blows

Cue 24   Black-out   (Page 80)
            Music

Cue 25   They all laugh   (Page 83)
            Music

MADE AND PRINTED IN GREAT BRITAIN BY
LATIMER TREND & COMPANY LTD PLYMOUTH

MADE IN ENGLAND